You'll Never Hairdr

CW00430767

Russell Paul Hughes

chipmunkapublishing

the mental health publisher

Russell Paul Hughes

Published by

Chipmunkapublishing

PO Box 6872

Brentwood

Essex CM13 1ZT

United Kingdom

http://www.chipmunkapublishing.com

Chipmunkapublishing gratefully acknowledge the support of Arts Council England.

You'll Never Make a Hairdresser

Foreword

'To dream the impossible dream, to reach for the unreachable star'

I had a dream once. Oh I know we all have dreams, but some people dream about being movie stars, millionaires or even walking on the moon. My dream in today's standards is within everyone's grasp; but to me, when I was younger I may as well have been dreaming to be the next big movie star. My dream was to become a hairdresser; not much to ask for, looking back.

Did I believe I would ever become a hairdresser?
No, because I believed that my working life had already been mapped out for me by my parents. How wrong I was, or should I say they were?

Did I think hairdressing would be an easy profession to go into?
I never really thought about it that way; I was just so determined that hairdressing was all I wanted to do. Looking back, I wasn't prepared for just how hard hairdressing would be.

Did I believe hairdressing would ever make me any money?
I never thought about money, I was too young to realise I needed money to get on in life. If you ask any stylist my age, they would also tell you there wasn't any money in hairdressing when we started out nearly thirty years ago; you became a hairdresser because you wanted to. It was your vocation. Today it's quite different because once you've completed your training, there's good money to be made.

People go through life dreaming of lots of wonderful things. I believe in the old saying that anything is possible, but what we must all remember is no one is going to give it to you on a plate; you have to be prepared to work. Work for whatever you want out of life and work hard for it. If you don't work hard at your dream, don't be too quick to judge those who have, when you see what they have achieved.

Do you have a dream?

If so, go and get it.

Russell Paul Hughes

You'll Never Make a Hairdresser

If at first you don't succeed

OK, so I lied. But Carol had been off school for weeks with a broken leg, and I said today I'd try and pull a sicky from school so I could spend the day with her.

'I don't feel well', I kept saying, following mum around the house as she was rushing around trying to get the rest of the kids ready for school.

'Well you're fucking going to school so go and get yourself ready'

I sat on the stairs trying to look as ill as possible. Every time she passed she'd shout out 'Get the fuck up and get ready. I'm telling you you're going in even if you're fucking dying, now come on'.

Slowly I started to get ready, still moaning about how ill I was until finally she gave in.

'OK then. But you'll have to come to town with me ill or not and let me find out you're fucking lying and you'll have your father to deal with. I'm not missing this fucking hair appointment for no one'.

'What, me?'

'Yeah you,' she shouted back.

'Now get ready to come into town with me'.

My plan wasn't going the way I'd wanted it to go. Sure I had managed to stay off school, but I didn't want to sit in a hairdressers all day and
I didn't even have time to go a few doors up and tell Carol, my best friend, what was going on.

'Quick kids, out the door. I'm going to miss this fucking bus. Now come on'.

After we'd got all the kids into school we jumped on the number 105 bus into Manchester city centre and it didn't take long for my travel sickness to kick in as it always did when I was in a car or bus. 'Mum I feel sick'

'Well what the fuck can I do? We'll be there in about half an hour'.

'But mum I'm going to be sick. Can we get off the bus at this stop and then get on the next one please?'

'Like fuck we can, and if you're sick on this fucking bus I'll kill ya'.

Too late! I'd vomited all over the floor and each time the bus turned so did the sick, swishing from side to side and making me feel even worse.

'You fucking dirty bastard' she kept saying over and over again. After we'd moved seats and I was feeling a bit better I had great pleasure in saying 'I told you I was ill!'

I remember the salon we went in was located in the downstairs of the building. I was feeling better by the time we got there but was still gutted that I was about to spend so much time in this hairdressers, but how unprepared I'd been for the experience I was about to encounter. I will never forget going downstairs and walking on that salon floor. I had never seen anything like it in my life. To me it was one of the most fascinating places I had ever visited. Mum was guided away by a young girl and I was told to wait in the reception area. The seat I chose to sit in was directly opposite a cut out in the wall, and I could see all the ladies sat in chairs having their hair done. I remember thinking the hairdressing salon was so beautiful. There was a fountain right in the middle of the reception area which amazed me because I had only ever seen a fountain outdoors, and that was in our local park and even then it was never working. I thought the salon staff were very glamorous and my eyes moved around quickly; from the girls cutting hair to the ones who were either making coffees or going to help customers with their coats. I loved it. It was another world to me and one that was so far away from the world I lived in.

Mum seemed to be there for hours and during my wait a couple of the staff came over to me to chat for a while. I think they must have felt sorry for me having to sit there all that time waiting for my mother, but little did they know I was loving every minute of it! A younger man came over and asked if I was fed up with waiting. I told him I didn't mind and with that he said I could go through to the staff room to have a drink with him. I jumped at the chance and walked across the salon floor as if I'd been working there for years. The look on my mother's face when she saw me was a picture! My memory of the staff room is that it was full of, what seemed to me, beautiful men and women. They were having their lunch and I remember they were very nice to me. They offered me a drink and food but I only took the drink. They were all talking about a customer's hair and what they were going to do with it. I wouldn't have minded if I never went home again and I never gave poor Carol a second thought. I was hooked and knew from that moment on I was going to be a hairdresser even if it killed me. When mum finally did appear she walked over to me in the reception.

'I bet you never thought I'd be that long did you? Well, it serves you right for being fucking ill. Next time you'll go to school won't you?'

She actually thought she had taught me a lesson but little did she know she had just given me the best thing she would ever give me in my whole life, and that was an introduction to hairdressing. Strangely, she told me to stand outside while she went and paid. At first I couldn't understand why but later on I soon found out it was because her hair cut had cost so much money. If I'd seen this and told Dad it would not only be me who'd have been ill because he'd have killed her!

I never found school easy. I don't know why and I don't want to blame anyone, but I found nearly ever topic so difficult to understand. I hated reading, writing, spelling, maths and sport. When I look back I thank God I found hairdressing because without it I don't know what I would have done. I was always being sent out of class for not doing as I was told and when I did try to tell the teachers that I simply couldn't do the work it only made things worse. There were some teachers who knew full well I struggled but insisted on asking me to read aloud to the whole class. I remember just standing there one day with the teacher shouting at me to read. The more I looked at the pages of this book the more I couldn't work any of it out, and so the tears slowly ran down my face. It was embarrassing but at the same time a relief when this teacher told me to get out of his class as I was 'thick as shit' and he couldn't do anything with me any more. I did tell my parents, but after laughing they just told me to piss off and go and play out. Some back up they were!

My father had his own business recycling waste paper which earned him a lot of money, but the majority of this went to support the local pub (or his office as he would say).When my brother Tommy left school he went straight to work for my dad. Everyone else in my family either worked for Smiths crisps or Paxo stuffing and I didn't want to work in a factory. The lucky ones got a job working in the Mr Kipling factory making cakes, and once you were in there I was told you had a job for life. My sister was considered one of the lucky ones when she started working there. I would go and meet her from work and see hundreds of people coming out after their shift. They wore white coats and had silly looking hats. Well if that was a job for life I'd think, God help me.

When I finally met up with Carol, I told her I was going to be a hairdresser when I left school and I told her about my day trip to Manchester.

'Why do you want to do that? Only queers do that job'

'No they don't'.

'Well my dad said they all are'.

'Well your dad's as thick as shit then innie'.

Carol shouted to her Mum in the living room; 'Have you heard this mum? Russell wants to be a hairdresser when he leaves school'.

'Oh lovely, I bet you'll be a bloody good one too. You can do my hair any time you want to love'.

Some months had passed when one day I heard my Mum shout upstairs to me; 'Carol's mother is here for you Russell'.

'OK, I'm coming down now'.

You'll Never Make a Hairdresser

As I made my way downstairs I was wondering what was wrong. Carol's mother had never been to my house before and I hoped Carol was all right.

'Hello Mrs Jackson'.

'Hiya love. I've just been to the shop and when I was passing the hairdressers I noticed that they had a sign in the window for a junior's job'.

I was just about to answer Mrs Jackson when I heard.

'Oh love he'll never make a fucking hairdresser as long as he's got a hole in his arse'. Yes, it was my mother back in the hallway offering her opinion as if it was needed. She'd obviously been listening from behind the living room door.

'Don't let him waste you're fucking time love, he's just not worth it'.

I couldn't believe what she had just said. Poor Mrs Jackson just stood there in shock and I knew she had never heard anything like that in all her life.

'But thanks for popping around love. See ya'.

With that said, mum was just about to shut the door but not before Mrs Jackson shouted;

'It's Mr Quinn's salon Russell'.

I couldn't believe how mum had spoken in front of Mrs Jackson and as I ran up stairs crying with embarrassment I could hear mum walking into the living room laughing.

'Have you heard this Val'? (Val was another neighbour from up the road). 'He wants to be a fucking hairdresser now the stupid bastard, getting all the fucking neighbours looking out for a job for him. Who the fuck does he think he is?'

Although I'd never asked Mrs Jackson to look out for any job for me I was so glad she did, and thought it was very nice of her to call around and tell me. Although I thought after this episode she'd never call again.

I couldn't wait to get to the hairdressing salon and after putting my best clothes on I set off. After finding the building I went in and was met by a very old man who I later found out was the barber. He was seventy years old and should have retired five years earlier, and as nice as he was to me I was not impressed so far. I mean what type of hair salon employed a seventy year old man? It certainly wasn't the type I was looking for!

'I've come about the job in the window' I said reluctantly.
'OK son, I'll go and get Mr Quinn for you. He's just upstairs in the ladies salon'.

Mmm, I was thinking, that's more like it, and I wished he'd invited me to go up with him just so I could have a look around. As the door opened upstairs I could hear the people talking and laughing and the noise of the hair dryers. This took me straight back to the salon in Manchester I'd visited with my mother. Before long I heard someone coming down the stairs.

'Hello, I'm Mr Quinn, how can I help you?'

'I've come about the job in the window'. I said with a big smile across my face.
'Oh I'm sorry son but the job I have on offer is for a young girl and not a boy. I am very sorry'.
And as he held the shop door open for me to leave he said. 'But thank you for coming'.

I couldn't believe it; I had never imagined it would have only been available for a girl. I left feeling sad, embarrassed and angry, and thinking what I would do next.

'Where have you been all dressed up?' asked my father when I returned home.

'Nowhere' I said as I started to make my way upstairs.

You'll Never Make a Hairdresser

'Your fucking father's talking to you; don't just go up to your room when he's asked you a question'.

'What?' I shouted back in retaliation.

'Well tell him where you've been'.

'I did mum. I said I've not been anywhere'.

There was no way I was going to tell them where I'd been because they would have found it hilarious.

I was passing Mr Quinn's a few weeks later when I noticed that the advert for the junior's job was still in the window. Having nothing to lose I decided to give it another go.

'Hi, is Mr Quinn in?' I said to the young girl as I walked up to the reception desk.

'What's it about?'

'I've come about the job in the window'.

'I'll just go and get him'.

Standing there waiting I felt quite alone and when she walked off to get Mr Quinn I regretted calling back. I was just about to walk out when I heard a voice.

'Hello again'.

'Hi'.

'Do you still want the job'?

'Yes please'.

'What's your name?'

'Russell'.

'Well Russell, I'm afraid the answer is still the same. I'm still looking for a young girl to take the job.

Thank you for your interest and I wish I could help you'.

'You can'.

'Oh. How?'

'You could give me the job. That would help me'.

'I'm sure it would, but as I'm looking for a girl it wouldn't help me now, would it?'

Once again I found myself following Mr Quinn to the salon door, only this time he was grinning.

'Maybe I could help you then Mr Quinn'.

'How's that then Russell?'

'I'll make you a new sign for your shop window'.

'Saying what? No boys need apply!'

'No! Only girls need apply'.

'He's got a point Mr Quinn' said the young girl who had come downstairs.

'Yes he has and thank you very much for pointing that out to me Russell; I'll correct it right away'.

'OK then, I'll see ya'.

'Bye Russell. Take care and thank you again for calling in'.

I wasn't feeling too bad by the time I left, but I'd made my mind up that if the job was still advertised the following week I'd go back and try again.
A week later I went back and as I was walking up to the salon door I

could see Mr Quinn stood looking out of the window. He watched me approach the salon and as I got nearer he ran to the door laughing. Which in turn made me laugh too!

'Will you ever take no for an answer?' he said with a big smile on his face.

'No' I insisted, smiling back at him.

'Anyway you're just as bad'.

'What do you mean?' he said as he opened the shop door further.

'Well you've still got the sign in the window, after all this time, and no-one wants your job, only me'.

'Well that's true so you'd better come in'.

Yes I remember thinking. I've got it.

'Come and sit over here and tell me why I should give you the job and why you want to be a bloody hairdresser so badly'.

I told him about the time I was off school and went to Manchester with my mother; I even told him the truth about how I told her I was unwell. He found this funny and started to laugh. I went on to explain that from that day on all I'd ever wanted was to be was a hairdresser.

'Are you still at school?'

'No I finished yesterday'.

'Do you know anything about hairdressing?'

'No'.

'It's long hours'.

'That's OK'.

'The pay isn't very good'.

'I don't mind'.

'At the end of all your training there is no guarantee you'll be a good hairdresser'.

'I will' I insisted.

Still smiling he said.

'You know what Russell, you just might. OK then, you can start next Tuesday and you'll have every Monday off.

I jumped up and down excitedly thanking him, and I was so pleased that my persistence had paid off. I couldn't believe I'd got the job, and apart from a little help from Mrs Jackson, I'd done it all on my own.

'That's OK. You work hard for me and you'll be OK, but before you go will you do something for me?'

'Yes sure, what is it?'

'Take down that bloody sign from the window before anyone else like you calls in!'

I jumped up, grabbed the sign and ran out of the shop.
I could hear Mr Quinn shouting in the background; 'Nine O'clock you start'. I laughed all the way home and could still not believe it. Me, Russell Hughes going to be a hairdresser. Ha!
I ran non stop all the way to my sister's flat. Allyson was a few years older then me, she may have been my sister but every one knew she was more like a mother to me. So much so that she was the one that I sent mother's day cards to. She lived as a lone parent with her young son after falling pregnant when she was just seventeen and had been told to leave our family home (a long story but one that will be written).

'That's great news, you'll be so good as a hairdresser, I know you will'.

You'll Never Make a Hairdresser

I knew she would be happy for me and I just wished that she too could be happy, but life had never been kind to her.

Before I went home to tell the rest of the family I went around to Carol's house.

'Hiya, come on in'.

'Is your mum in?'

'Why?'

'Oh I just wanted to tell her something'.

'She's in the living room, come in'.

As I walked in the living room both Carol's parents were sat there. I didn't want to say anything at first because of Carol's father sitting there but then I thought, oh sod him.

'Mrs Jackson, I have called around to say thank you for letting me know about the job in the hairdressers' I started.

'Oh that's OK love, have you been to see them yet?'

'Yes, I've been three times'.

'Why three times love?'

I went on to explain what had happened with Mr Quinn and when I finally finished my story she got up and gave me a big hug.

'Oh that's great news love, just great'.

Carol's dad didn't look too pleased and just sat there looking me up and down in a disapproving way; but what the hell; I was happy and didn't give a shit. Now I had to go home and break the news to the rest of the family.

I'm told that I was six weeks old when I was finally allowed home from hospital. Waiting for me and my mother at home was my older sister Allyson who was five years old and my older Brother Tommy who was eighteen months; and of course there was my father. To this day I still don't have an explanation of what happened, but my birth mother had planned it that only I was going over the threshold into the family home that day. Somewhere along the way my mother had made other plans in which there was no room for me nor the rest of the family. She passed me to my father and got back into the taxi never to return.

After some time my father found help and companionship through his sister's best friend (hello step mother!). From then on our up bringing was to be far different from that of our friends, but as my elder sister always said, at least we were together. Even now I don't believe that an only child would ever have coped. Over the twenty or so years their relationship lasted, my father and step mother went on to have another five children after which my father left to take up residence with another woman. By this time me, my brother and my sister had well and truly been evicted from the nest.

There was so much laughter in the room when I told the family about my job and this mockery left me standing there feeling like a clown in the middle of the ring at an opening night at the circus. I hadn't expected anything less, and took comfort in the fact that I wasn't going to be following the family tradition and working in some factory.

I had met Mr Quinn a few times now so I could not understand why I was so nervous, but looking back it was the week before my first hairdressing job and I didn't really know what to expect. Shit, I remember thinking, I need my own hair cut, but I couldn't ever remember going to a hairdressers or barbers as a customer. I had an auntie who had been cutting my hair from god knows when, so it was only right she did it one last time for me.

I set off to work feeling so smart wearing my new black pants, white shirt and my new black dickey bow that I'd just bought from the local market; well I did want to look like the guys in the hairdressing salons in Manchester (remember it was 1982 and this was high fashion at the time!)

You'll Never Make a Hairdresser

As I walked into the salon I was greeted by a young girl.

'Hi, I'm Mandy' she said.

'Hello' I said. 'I'm Russell'.

'Mmm, I've heard all about you Russell and how many times you kept coming in for the job. It's not that good you know.

She turned and headed upstairs shouting at me behind her.

'Well come on then, you'd better come on up'.

'This is the ladies' salon' she explained. 'The guys have their hair cut downstairs with Arthur. He's leaving soon because he's been here for bloody years. He's getting on a bit so try and stay out of his way, he doesn't like new faces and believe me he's seen a few'.

'What's that smell?' I said as she was showing me around.
'Oh that's perm lotion; you'll get used to that. All the old bids have perms here'.

'Old bids?'

'Yeah, this salon's full of them'

'It's not quite what I was expecting'

'Well you're free to leave' she said unsympathetically.

'Oh God no, it's took me ages to get this job'

'I don't know why you wanted it so much?' she questioned. 'It's not fucking Vidal Sassoon but I suppose it's the nearest you'll get in Wythenshawe'

Along one side of the salon there were windows hung with lace that looked as if they hadn't seen a washing machine in years. All along the opposite wall were rows and rows of dryer banks (these are chairs with larger hood dryers attached to the back of them) and each dryer had its own ashtray in the arm of the chair (How things

17

have changed).

There were trolleys all over the place, all overflowing with different coloured hair rollers, most covered in bits of the last customer's hair and what looked like multi-coloured cobwebs hanging from the handles of the trolleys turned out to be hair nets full of holes.

'Come on through here, this is where all the hairdressing is done'

You must be joking I thought. This room was just as bad, with chairs that were so old they must have been made in nort plonk.

'I told you it wasn't Vidal's'

'Yer but - '

'Oh come on' she interrupted 'this is where they get shampooed, then you take them over to one of the chairs; but don't worry, most of the ladies have been coming here that long they'll tell you what to do and where they like to sit'.

'How long have you been working?'
Before she'd had chance to answer my question the salon door opened and a queue of old ladies began to enter.

'Speak of the devil' said Mandy. 'They don't even let you get in and have a cup of tea'.

It was like a mad granny race and I just managed to get out of the way before being trampled over by a load of O A P's, all heading towards the wash basins that looked equally as old, and as though they might fall off the wall at any minute.

'Now come on Mrs Brown' said Mandy as she tried to slow down one of her clients. 'We don't want any accidents now do we'?

Several of the other ladies had decided to help themselves to the hairdressing gowns that were hung on the wall with big nails.

'Come on now ladies' Mr Quinn shouted as he walked into the room accompanied by a younger looking woman. When I say younger, she must have been in her forties, but compared to the rest of the women in the room she was a young chick.

'Hello Russell' said Mr Quinn. 'Glad you made it, and sorry for shouting but you'll learn half of these old dears are stone deaf.'

'I'm Barbara' said the other woman who was with him.

I just stood there in shock and from my facial expression Barbara must have picked up on this.

'Come on now ladies, settle down' she shouted. 'This is Russell, he's come to work here today, so don't bloody scare him off before he gets started'.

Where was this nice salon I thought I was going to work in, and where were all the beautiful staff and clients I had remembered from a few years ago? I felt as if I had just walked into an old folk's home, and looking at the rest of the staff I was well over-dressed standing there looking like the head waiter in a restaurant.

I quickly learned to drop the dickey bow and within a few days I was well into my new job. The old dears loved me and I had started to get used to them as well. I soon learnt that each one of them had a story to tell, and I could have sat with them for hours and hours listening to their life stories, but there was always someone else who needed to be shampooed or be put under the dryer, or who was waiting for their rollers to be taken out. I was learning so much from Mr Quinn's salon, but I wasn't entirely sure it was what I needed or wanted to learn. Was this really hairdressing or was it just filling a gap in the hairdressing market that no one else wanted to do? Although I was glad the salon was there catering for all these pensioners, I began to realise that this type of salon was not enough for me. I still couldn't get the memory of the first salon that I'd seen out of my head.

Within a few weeks Mr Quinn called me into his office which was on the landing at the top of the stairs. I remember it being so small that you couldn't really describe it as a room. He told me how well I was doing and he was so glad that he had taken me on.

What an understatement I thought, considering I was spending my days running around his salon like a blue arse fly. If I wasn't shampooing or cleaning up I'd be doing towels, and if I wasn't working on the salon floor then I was the poor sod who was sent out to get all the staff lunches; and even those old net curtains got to see the inside of a washing machine!

The kitchen to the salon was downstairs, which meant that each time someone wanted a drink I had to keep going up and down the stairs. Usually by the time I'd asked each of the ladies what they wanted to drink and how many sugars they took, and had got down the stairs I'd forgotten who had asked for what. I eventually started writing the orders in a note pad to the amusement of the rest of the staff, but it wasn't them running up and down the bloody stairs all day!

In between working for my father my older brother worked on a farm in Wythenshawe and was earning roughly £130.00 a week. One of my younger sisters worked at Kipling's factory and earned between £110.00 and £120.00 a week, and another sister worked in the paxo factory which earned her about £105.00 a week. It didn't seem fair to me that from the £17.50 a week I brought home I was paying the same amount of keep as my brother and sisters which was set at £10 a week. On top of this if we wanted a bath we were charged an additional 50p towards the water and heating bill, and if we wanted to play our music that again was a 50p charge towards the cost of the electricity meter. So my weekly bill came to at least £17.00 a week before I'd left the bleeding house. I decided it was time to call a family meeting. The only time you could catch my father at home sober was on a Sunday morning when he was doing his Sunday breakfast. So one Sunday I called everyone into the living room to hear what I had to say.

To date this is still the quickest meeting I have ever had in my life. All I suggested was that I should pay a little less keep based on the fact that my wage was lower than the rest of the family. No sooner had I said my piece when mum jumped up and said

'You wanted to be a fucking poxy hairdresser not us, that's the end of this fucking meeting; now fuck off the lot of you.'

I don't know how I ever managed to survive on that income but somehow I did. The old dears would give me tips but unfortunately 5p here and there didn't get me very far. I decided that I needed to do something else or get some additional work. I had been working for Mr Quinn for about six months when he told me he was planning to have a few days off and that he was going to see a hotel that was up for sale in Llandudno. He asked me if I would mind taking the salon takings home with me on the Wednesday, Thursday and Friday evening and bring them to him on the Saturday morning when he returned. I was OK with that because I only lived up the road and it wasn't as though I would get mugged on the way home or anything.

On the Tuesday night I bagged up the takings and put them in the bottom drawer in my bedroom as soon as I got home. I did the same on the Wednesday night, Thursdays night and again on Friday, making sure I didn't tell anyone they were there. When Saturday morning came I went to get the money only to discover I was one bag short.

I realised it was Wednesday's money that was missing; that was the salons half day closing and I knew the takings had been low. I remembered that we had only taken £27.50 but that was not the point, where had it gone? Frantically I ran down stairs shouting mum and dad.

'It's gone, it's gone'

But they had never known the money was there. No one had. I was shaking and sweating

'Oh God what am I going to do?'

All I got back from my parents was how much of a daft bastard I was for bringing it home in the first place. Great help!

Walking to work that day I didn't know what I was going to do or say. Suddenly I heard the beeping of a car. I think I nearly shit myself as Mr Quinn pulled over to offer me a lift. As I got into his car I felt sick.

'Hello Russell how are you?'

'Mmm, I'm OK'.

'What's wrong'?

'Wrong? Nothing'.

'Come on you can tell me'.

I'm sure he must have thought I was having trouble at home again. I wish it had been that, I thought to myself. I plucked up the courage and told him the whole thing but by the time I was getting towards the end I'd started to cry.

'I swear to you Mr Quinn I did not take it, I swear'. I repeated this over and over again.

Mr Quinn pulled his car over and I thought he was going to ask me to get out and go home.

'I want you to calm down Russell. I know you didn't take that money and like I believe you I want you to believe me when I say this. You were on your way to work when I picked you up were you not?'

'Yes'

'Well there you are then. If you had taken that money you wouldn't be coming back to work now would you? I might have only known you for a short time Russell, but I know you didn't take that money'.

I offered to pay back Mr Flynn £1.00 a week to which he agreed and as far as I was aware he never told anyone about the missing money and I certainly didn't.

By now the staff were letting me put rollers in for some of the ladies which meant they got a reduction off their bill and which was great for me because before long I was getting a busy column.

'Russell' I heard one of the stylists shout. 'Would you take Edna out of the dryer'?

You'll Never Make a Hairdresser

Edna was a nice old lady and on this particular day she had treated herself to a perm. As I made my way around to the dryer banks I could see Edna sat there. Bless her I thought, like most of the older ladies she's fallen asleep under the dryer.

'OK Edna' I prompted.

After no response I slowly lifted the hood dryer. 'Edna' I said 'come on love you're ready to come out now 'but still there was nothing. The other ladies sitting either side of Edna just smiled at me as I continued to lift the hood dryer off her. Just as I did, I got the shock of my life when poor Edna fell forwards towards me.

Trying to take control of the situation I kept one hand on the hood of the dryer to stop it falling back down and used the other to try and prop Edna up. Realising what had happened, and to add to my anxiety, the ladies sitting next to Edna started to let out high pitched screams all over the salon. Their shrill cries set the other customers off and before long the whole fucking salon was in mayhem.

The other members of staff came running around the corner to investigate the commotion; some one was shouting to call for an ambulance, ladies were frantically trying to free themselves from under the dryers, and me; well I was still stood holding the hood of the dryer with one hand and a dead Edna with the other when Mr Quinn came shouting around the corner.

'What have you done?'

I shouted back to him 'I only lifted the fucking dryer and she was dead'.

In my whole history of hairdressing this is the only occasion on which I have ever sworn on the shop floor and believe me, under the circumstances it was called for. The ambulance arrived and once poor Edna had been taken away the police began to question us all. It turned out Edna had had a heart attack but all Mr Quinn was bothered about was whether he was going to get his rollers back. (He never did). Experiencing Edna's death was more than enough for me and I decided that I'd worked long enough with the old ladies. I did feel sad leaving my first job, and despite the fast pace of the salon I had managed to learn so much. I had also realised that there was far more to hairdressing that I still had to learn, and sadly I wasn't going to advance much further if I were to stay; I was still young and didn't want to become another Mr Quinn. Looking back I can truthfully say he was the best boss I've ever had (and I've had a few). I didn't see very much of the staff from Mr Quinn's salon after I had left. This changed however about six months later when I was packing my belongings to move them out of my parents' house and into my own flat.

As I was carrying an old chest of drawers down the stairs I noticed something on the landing floor. To my amazement it was the money bag I had stashed there months before when I'd been given the responsibility of looking after the takings. I couldn't believe that after all this time I'd found the missing money which I had convinced myself that someone in the house had taken. Gladly I realised how wrong I was. Once the van was full of all my belongings I asked the driver to take me straight to Mr Quinn's salon. As per usual Mr Quinn was stood there looking out of his salon window. After he'd greeted me with a big hello I showed him what I'd discovered and recalled the way I'd found it.

I wanted him to know I hadn't taken it and neither had any of my family as I had thought. To prove its authenticity the bag still contained the old till receipt still with his £27.50!

'Russell, I told you then and I'll tell you again I never thought for one second that you had taken that money'.

As I passed him the envelope which contained his money he said 'No Russell, this is yours, you've already paid me back remember?'

We sat chatting for a while. It was nice to see him and the salon again even if nothing inside had changed. I was sure the net curtains hadn't been washed since I had left and I bet myself they'd stay that way until the next hard working junior came along. As I left I placed the envelope of cash somewhere that I knew Mr Quinn would find it. After the amount of time I had spent telling him I hadn't taken his money, I was not going to take it now!

Julie was a friend of my mother's and to this day I'll never know what they had in common. Julie had worked all her life as a hairdresser, was married, lived in a nice three bed semi and had two children later on in life. But what was even better for me was she had her own salon. My mother had never worked a day in her life, had that many kids she couldn't control them, lived in a council house in not such a great area and had as she would often quote 'never got a pot to piss in'. The day I knew Julie was calling I was ready with a plan worked out in my head. I watched through the window until I saw her soft top car pull up, and then hurried down the stairs. I just managed to meet Julie as we were walking through the gate.

'You look very smart' she said. 'Where are you off to?'

'I'm going looking for a new job'

'Didn't you like hairdressing?'

I briefly explained about why I'd left Mr Quinn's.

'Why don't you come and work in my salon?' she suggested. 'I can only pay you £27.50 a week. What were you on before?'.

'The same' I lied.

Well what's one little lie? I wasn't going to tell her that I'd only been getting £17.50 now was I? My plan had worked; a better salon, better training and more pay. What more could a young man ask for?

'Well you don't have to go out now so you can go and put the kettle on for me and your mother. I'll see you bright and early tomorrow and your day off will be a Monday'

As I walked towards the living room with their drinks I could hear mother saying

'You'll be sorry you took him on Julie. I'm telling you now'.

Julie just looked at me and smiled. I had already told her what I could and couldn't do when I'd 'bumped into her' outside, and she seemed more than pleased with that. Julie knew as well as I did that mum didn't have a clue what she was talking about.

Julie's salon was a lot further away from home, but the extra money helped pay towards my bus fare when the weather was bad. There were many occasions that I still had no money and would end up having to walk for an hour before I even started work, but I knew on my first day it would all be worth it. The salon was bigger, trendier and had a younger clientele.

It was 1982 and Charlie's Angels were a big hit on the television, and many of the girls I knew aspired to be like one of the three characters from the show. It came as no surprise to me when I walked in the house one night when my mother asked

'Oh our Russell, will you make me look like Farrah Fawcett-Majors?'

'Yes' I agreed. 'I'll do it tomorrow night for you when I've finished work'

'Do what?' she shouted.

'A perm. You'll need a perm if you want to look anything like her mum'

But inside I was thinking you'll need more then a fucking perm to look like her. Although perms were very much in fashion in the eighties I had never actually done one. I'd watched many being done and felt confident that it wouldn't be that hard to do. What could go wrong?

Now anyone reading this book who remembers Farrah Fawcett-Majors will remember that as well as being an actress she was also a popular pin up. She was very beautiful and had the most fantastic hair which was long and blonde with big beautiful bouncy curls. I was sure she must have had a perm to get all that body in her hair, but the only thing I was unsure of was which size perm rollers to use. (Having years of experience I now know that the bigger the roller the bigger the curl).

You'll Never Make a Hairdresser

It took me hours to get all the small perm rollers in my mother's hair, this being because her hair was so long and secondly because I had never done a perm before.

'It fucking stinks in here' said Dad as he walked into the kitchen.

'Hey Ed, I'm gonna look like Farrah Fawcett tonight, aren't I our Russ?'

'Yep' I agreed just as I was getting my last roller in.

'Right we have to leave it for about an hour now' I guessed.

'A fucking hour! I've never had to leave it on that long before in the salons' she complained.

'But you're not in a salon are ya?'

'An hour seems a long fucking time to me'

'Leave him, he knows what he's doing. He's the poxy fucking hairdresser remember'

'Thanks dad' I said. 'I'll be outside talking to Denise'.

'Fuck Denise' exclaimed Mum. 'You'd better keep an eye on this perm'.

'It's a new perm called an acid perm. It sounds bad but I'm told it's kinder to your hair. You'll get lovely curls with this perm mum'.

I hadn't been at the door that long when mum came over to me and Denise who was my friend from North Wales. I'd met her at her sister's house who lived a few doors down. I would often baby sit for her sister's children if I needed more cash so it was quite a regular occurrence.

'This perm has been on over an hour now'

'Look mum, I'm the hairdresser'

I loved saying that to her, especially in front of my friend Denise who thought being a hairdresser was so cool.

'I'll come and check it in a minute. Go and wait in the kitchen, I'm coming in now'

I saw Denise off and then went back into the kitchen, bearing in mind I didn't actually know what I was looking for. By the time I had got into the kitchen mum had her head over the kitchen sink rinsing her hair.

'Mum I was going to look at it first.'

'Fuck that' she said. 'Hairdresser or no hairdresser, I know this fucking perm has been on long enough.'

After the neutraliser had been on for ages it was time to take the rollers out.

Now this is the bit that I was good at as I'd had plenty of practice in work. I took one roller out at the bottom near the nape of her neck because I knew this was the longest part of her hair, but as the hair left the roller it didn't fall into the big bouncy curl I thought it would. Instead it shot up to the nape of her neck and sat there like a bunch of pubic hair. Mmm I thought, may be the next one will come out big and beautiful? No chance! Neither did the next nor the next one after that. By the time I had removed half a head of rollers I realised that what should have been a cascade of curls was in fact a matt of tight frizz. By this time mum was saying.

'Thanks for doing this for me Russell, I've always loved her hair. Oh and wait till your father sees it'

I felt sick. By now I had taken all the back curlers out and my hands were starting to shake and to make matters worse Dad walked into the kitchen.

'I don't know about Farrah Fawcett Majors, but from where I'm standing you look more like fucking Michael Jackson to me'

Thanks dad!

You'll Never Make a Hairdresser

'You what?' she said reaching to her shoulders in the hope of feeling big bouncy curls but instead she felt a frizzy matter that had once been her hair. She jumped up and before she'd even got to the mirror to inspect it herself she was shouting.

'I'll fucking kill him'
That was my cue. Once she'd started to scream I began to race up the stairs, only to hear her close behind me screaming.

'I'll fucking kill you' she continued.

I just managed to pull the lock across the back of the toilet door when she started to kick it.

'You're dead! You're dead! You're fucking dead!'

I didn't know whether to laugh or cry, but one thing I knew I wasn't going to escape without injury.

'Dad, Dad' I shouted.

What else could I do? One more kick on that door and the fucking lock was gonna go. Dad got to the top of the stairs and started to laugh, which was the worst possible thing anyone could have done in view of the situation.

'Right you fucking little bastard'

Bang! That's it. It'd gone.

The force of the door pushed me back against the wall. She was desperately trying to get her hand in between the door and the wall so she could hit me, and in fear I continued screaming.

'Dad, Dad'.

'I'm gonna fucking kill him' is all she could shout.

In the middle of all this commotion we heard a knock at the door. To all our horrors it was Denise, back to see how my mother's perm had gone.

I didn't have much street cred but the little I'd acquired had just flown right out of the toilet window. Mum took great delight in telling Denise how shit I was at hairdressing. Dad just said it was her own fault for letting me do it in the first place when I had so little experience. Looking back it was funny, but I'm sure my mother thought otherwise!

You'll Never Make a Hairdresser

Mobile

Living on one of the biggest council estates in Britain there wasn't going to be any trouble getting people to practice my hairdressing on. Most of the people I knew had been having their hair cut by their mothers (or in my case my aunty) all their lives. I needed a way of generating additional income as I knew the wage for hairdressing wouldn't be good to begin with. I also knew that mobile hairdressing wasn't going to earn me a fortune either, but seeing as I had never picked up a pair of scissors in my life it was going to give me some much needed practice. My customers didn't need to know this of course, and as long as they knew I was working in a hairdressing salon they wouldn't question me any further. I reached the decision that I wouldn't tell them I was only cleaning all day and wouldn't be starting to learn how to cut for at least another year.

Within the first week of me starting work as a junior I had unsuccessfully attempted a perm on my mother's hair which we now know was my first real disaster. Although I didn't get the Farah Fawcett look quite right, looking at my mother's hair you'd think I'd been doing Diana Ross' hair for years! Getting the guys to have their hair cut was easy because most of them didn't want to pay too much money and didn't really care what they looked like anyway. It was good training for me nevertheless, even if all the cuts looked the same. The older guys were better to practise on because they were happy to just sit in their kitchens with an old tea towel around their necks and let me hack away.

'Do whatever you like son' they'd say with confidence. And most of the time I always did!

I could make a fifty year old guy look thirty, but unfortunately I had the reverse effect on the younger guys and the poor eighteen year olds often ended up looking more like thirty by the time I'd finished. But for a few quid there wasn't much they could say.

After my mother had told almost everybody on the estate about how bad her perm had turned out I wasn't asked to do many of the women, and when I was it was usually for someone who was either house bound or dying.

'Russell' Mum shouted one day.

'What?'

'Flo's here'

'OK, I'm coming'

Flo's husband had just died and mum had told Flo that I'd do her hair for her before her husband's funeral, although what I was going to do to her I had no idea.

'Hi Flo' I said walking into the kitchen. Flo didn't have much hair, and what she did have was very thin.

'Hiya love. Your mum said you'd do my hair for Bill's funeral' she said tearfully.

'Oh Flo, come on now, Bill wouldn't want this now would he?' said mum, passing her another glass of Q C sherry.

Flo decided that she wanted some Hi Lights which were usually applied through a streaking cap.(Not a lot of hairdressers were using foils at this time). As a newcomer to the profession I didn't have a streaking cap, so I decided that a plastic carrier bag would do the same job. After finding a way to hold the bag in place I started to pull Flo's hair through using a crocheting hook.

'Blonde Flo?' I asked, putting the 60 vol bleach all over.

'Oh please love' she said slowly, getting more and more pissed with my mother.

'Right, that's you done' I said after clipping another carrier bag over the already swelling bleach.

'I'm going to my room for a bit, I'll come and see how you're getting on later'.

It wasn't long before I heard mum running up the stairs shouting me.

You'll Never Make a Hairdresser

'What?' I asked as I meet her half way.

'You'd better get down here to Flo now' she said in a low voice so Flo could not hear her.

'All that fucking white stuff is dripping all over the place' (The white stuff was the bleach)

'OK I'm on to it. Chill out'

I walked into the kitchen not wanting Flo to know I did not have a clue what I was doing.

'Time to wash this off now Flo' I said as I started to move the stack of dirty pots that had been left in the kitchen sink from tea.

'OK Flo?'

As I began washing her hair I could see that there wasn't much of her own colour left. Because her hair was so fine I had unknowingly pulled the whole lot through the plastic carrier bag and because the bag had been sat on her head protecting her scalp, it had left a rim of her darker colour which made her look like she desperately needed her roots doing.

The look on my mum's face said it all! I think this was the only time mum had ever stuck up for me when she told Flo how nice her hair looked blonde. It was only because she didn't want to hurt her feelings or upset her before Bill's funeral that she went along with this. Flo seemed OK with the colour but I believe this was because she was half pissed on sherry by the time I'd finished. Needless to say Mum went mad when Flo went home.

'I only asked you to make her look and feel better for Bill's funeral, not make her look like fucking Marilyn Monroe.' Dad disagreed with this by saying she looked more like Myra Hindley. I thought she looked like neither, but one thing I did learn from that experience was never to use a plastic carrier bag again to streak someone's hair.

With these disasters behind me I was actually starting to do some good work, and it didn't take long before I was building up a good clientele.

In fact things picked up so well that I was finishing work in the salon at five and going out to do mobile work until midnight.

It was hard work, but I needed both the money and the experience, and what else would I have been doing anyway? The people on the estate might not have had much money, but they made the most of the conditions in which they lived and knew how to have a good laugh. I'd often cut someone's hair only to be asked afterwards 'Can I give you the money when my old man gets in from work?'

What could I say? I'd already done their hair but I knew I'd probably never get the money from them. It was silly really because they could never ask me again, but that didn't seem to bother them.

Whatever the weather or time of day I always travelled from one mobile job to the next on foot. I had never been able to afford driving lessons, and owning a car was certainly out of the question, and because of this I desperately needed something in which I could carry all my hairdressing tools, so the day I saw an old lady pulling a shopping trolley I knew I'd found a solution to my problem!

The trolley I bought was green check on a black frame. Everyone I knew took the piss out of me but I had to have it, it was the only luxury I could afford and it made my job so much easier.

Technology at this time had just progressed to the video recorder and not many families owned one, but those that did found that their houses were forever being robbed. The culture of stealing from your neighbours was rife in this part of Manchester and this extended to the kids as well. Families who owned videos would invite their kids' friends in to watch a video and it was not uncommon for some kids to then call back later that night when everyone was in bed to rob the video recorder!

I was out working mobile one evening when a police car slowly drove past me. The policemen inside seemed to be looking hard at me as they passed but I thought nothing of it and continued on my way. A few minutes later they were back again, only this time they pulled up just in front of me. It was about seven thirty and I was on my way to do Mrs Greenwood's colour.

You'll Never Make a Hairdresser

'What's in the shopping trolley?' the officer asked.

'Hairdressing things'

'What do you mean Hairdressing things? Open the trolley up'.

His colleague started to get out of the car as I was unzipping my trolley.
Smiling to him the first policeman said.

'He said he's got hairdressing things in here'

Because Mrs Greenwoods was having a colour this meant my trolley was filled to the brim with all my tools.

'Empty it' the copper insisted.

'Why, it's only my hairdressing things?'

'Fucking empty it now' he repeated.

I started to take the top things out of the trolley but obviously not at a pace that was quick enough for the boys in blue.

'Move' said one of the policemen pushing me out of the way.

Grabbing my trolley he picked it up, turned it upside down and started shaking everything out onto the pavement. To add insult to injury the other policeman started to push my things around with his feet.

There were pins, perm rollers, hair rollers and combs; you name it, I had it, and now they were all over the fucking pavement.

'What the fuck are you doing with all this?'

Just as I started to explain one of the policemen picked up my tail comb which had a long metal thin spike sticking out of one end.

'We're looking for videos' he said 'but this is even better, we can have you for carrying an offensive weapon'

'Offensive weapon! It's my fucking tail comb for doing people's hair'.

'Not any more it's not'.

Walking to their car with my comb they said. 'If we see you again with one of these we'll take you in'.

So there I was, left picking up all my things and thinking what a joke it was. I was only trying to earn some extra money doing mobile hairdressing and being threatened with an arrest if I was caught with my equipment again. That same couple of policemen must have stopped me ten times over, and each time they made me empty out my shopping trolley and each time they would take away my tail combs. After some time they failed to find them, and I remember the policeman saying

'It took you a while but you're a good boy now'

I just smiled back, thinking 'fuck you mate they're in my sock!'

The phone in our house was forever being cut off, which made mobile hairdressing even more difficult for me. Even when the phone was connected I would never give out our number because I knew it wouldn't be long before it was cut off again. Nobody had the luxury of a mobile phone in the eighties, so most of the mobile hairdressing I got was from word of mouth which today I believe is still the best form of advertising.

The salon I worked in didn't allow its staff to do mobile hairdressing outside of work and if they had ever found out what I was up to I would have been given the sack. It was the fact that the wages in hairdressing were so poor that I was forced into mobile work, but I did learn so much from doing mobile and managed to get most of my fuck ups out of the way!

There were so many clients that did ask if their salon stylist would consider doing their hair at home, but it was just not worth it; neither for the client nor the hairdresser. If a customer had really wanted a mobile hairdresser there were plenty of them around.

You'll Never Make a Hairdresser

For a lot of people their visit to the salon is an enjoyable morning or afternoon out, and this was especially so for the older clients whose visit was sometimes the only contact they had apart from the dog or cat.

Although it's considered very bad practice for a stylist to take clients away from the salon in which they work in I have known many stylists that have. There are plenty of clients to go around everyone, and hairdressers should always remember the saying 'Don't bite the hand that feeds you'. In my history of hairdressing I have seen many a good hairdresser out of work because they have taken clients from their salon to do them at home. Not only did it cost them the trust they had established with their boss, but news of their behaviour quickly spreads to other salon owners who wouldn't take the risk of employing them.

Although people might believe that one hair salon is the rival to the next hair salon up the road this is not always true. Sure, I have worked in hairdressing salons in the past that have told me that I was not allowed to talk to any of the staff from any other surrounding salons, but generally this is not the norm. I always found such rivalry a bit silly, especially when it extended to the hairdressing college as well. All the juniors went to the same hairdressing college, and, depending on which salon they were from, some would talk to you and others would just look over as if to say I know you work in that shit salon up the road! More often than not salon managers who work in the same locality do get on with each other and have all employed the same stylists at some time.

My best friend Carol had a telephone and it wasn't long before I had made arrangements for her to take my mobile hair appointments on the promise that for every client she booked she got paid fifty pence, which was quite a bit for a seventeen year old back then. All she had to do was write the customers' names and phone numbers down and I did the rest.
This worked well, but Carol soon got fed up but thankfully her mother agreed to take over on the same rate of pay but with the addition of free hairdo's. This was a good arrangement for us both, but the only down side for me would be when she took bookings that were miles away. I must have walked hundreds of miles during

that time of my life, pulling along that bloody shopping trolley full of equipment, which wasn't an easy thing to do in Wythenshawe.

It seemed like I had been doing mobile work for years before I finally started to get the younger clientele I had been aiming for since day one. After the disaster with my mother's perm and the way she went on about it to every soul she came in contact with it wasn't surprising that my popularity took some time to get established!

Looking back I can see now that they were right, but at the time all I wanted to do was to cut someone's hair. It had never once occurred to me that I actually wasn't capable of it, nor that I might make someone look a complete mess. My customers never seemed completely assured or comforted by my philosophy on hairdressing that mistakes will always grow back!

One day Carol's mother took a telephone appointment from a lady from Didsbury which was quite a long way from where I lived.
I'd travelled through there on the bus so I had a rough idea where it was.

'Who is she?' I said to Carol's mother

'I don't know love. Are you going to go?'

'Yeah, but I'll have to get the bus'

'50p then love, come on that's another one I got you'

After giving Carol's mum her money I went to the telephone box to call the customer to find out what she wanted and when she'd like her hair done. It turned out she wanted a cut and blow and she went on to tell me where to get off the bus and which directions to take to get to her house. All this for £3.50 I thought; well £3.00 because I'd just given 50p away. Was it really worth it?

I stood outside and looked up at the house in Didsbury, having never seen anything so nice in all my life. It was certainly nothing like the council houses on the estate that I had just travelled from. I rang the door bell and introduced myself to her husband who answered the door. He invited me in and asked me to wait for his wife in the dining room. A dining room was not something I was familiar with, and on entering I felt like I had just walked on to the set of Dallas or some other TV show.

There was a huge wooden table in the centre of the room surrounded by a number of chairs which was truly a world away from my life. Sure, we had a table in the kitchen that seated two people but the rest of us had to eat our dinner off our knees. It wasn't an ideal place to eat from, but was much better than sitting at our small kitchen table below a rack which was always full of dripping wet washing. If you weren't quick enough at eating your food you would end up piss wet though.

Looking back today the house in Didsbury was just a three bed semi with a table and chairs in a separate room, but at the time it was so much more to me. It was what I wanted, a home of my own, a home with my own dining room with a table and at least six chairs.

Eventually a lovely looking woman came into the room wearing a dressing gown. She introduced herself to me and told me she was a school teacher. She had seen a cut I had done for one of her colleagues and liked it so much she asked for my telephone number. To say I was gob smacked was an under statement. Here I was stood in this magnificent house with a school teacher who wanted me to cut her hair. The last time I had stood in front of a teacher was when he was telling me to get out of the class room because I was thick as shit. How my life was changing just by having the skill of cutting hair.

My previous experience of teachers had had a bad effect on me. I never thought I'd ever be stood in a teacher's house, never mind cutting their hair. Things were looking up.

On her instruction I followed her upstairs and into her bedroom. I noticed she locked the bedroom door behind us.

'Is this OK over here?

'There's more light here' she said as she sat down in front of the bedroom mirror within the bay window.

'Yes' I agreed as I started to get my things ready. For some reason I felt uneasy, but wasn't sure whether it was the 'teacher thing' that was still stuck in the back of my mind. I tried to put this to one side and listened as she described how she wanted her hair styling.

'Do you mind if I just slip this gown off? she asked unexpectedly. 'I don't want to get hair on it'.

Before I could say jack flash it was off and she was just sat there in front of her bedroom mirror without a stitch on apart from a towel around her waist! I've cut my fingers a few times in my hairdressing life but how I ever walked out of that house with a finger left on my hand I'll never know. I mean what the hell was she doing? What did she want me to do or say? Whatever it was she never got it! I was so glad to get out of that house and I vowed never to go back.
She could stick her big bleeding house with her poxy dining room. If that's what was hiding behind the nice front doors of all those houses, they could stick it.

I'd been working in a salon for some time when one of the girls came into the staff room and said that an old guy had phoned to ask if someone could call to his home and cut his hair .This type of request wasn't uncommon, and if the caller was already a client and was maybe under the weather for example, then a stylist, with permission from the salon manager, would call and do the client's hair. On this occasion the request came from a man who had never been to the salon before and therefore no one was permitted to go, even if they had wanted to. Strangely week on week the same guy kept calling the salon asking for a home appointment. Eventually the salon owner offered the opportunity for one of the staff to go, but no one was keen on the idea of it. Being a gent's cut there wasn't enough money in it for anyone, but by contrast had it been a perm or colour they'd all have been fighting over it.

'I'll go then' I offered.

With that I went off to call this guy up and tell him I'd call after work on my way home. I must have been about twenty two or twenty three at this time, and had established myself as a busy stylist on the salon floor; I was also married with my first child. Before leaving work I called my wife, telling her I'd be about half an hour late home from work. I knew it wouldn't take me too long to cut his hair, and as I had to pass his house on the way home the job hadn't appeared to be too much of an inconvenience. When I got to the house a little old man opened the door and invited me in. I was struck immediately by the filth in the house and a stench so strong it made me feel sick.

'Come on in son'.

He led me into his kitchen where I was greeted by a pan sitting on the cooker with mould floating on the top of the water. What looked like the remains of boiled potatoes lay dormant in the pan. The pots in the sink looked like they had been there for years, and the work tops were covered in spiders' webs. As I walked over to a chair I could feel my feet sticking to the floor and could hear a ripping noise as I lifted up one foot to put in front of the other. It was so bad that all I could think of was why was this man living in such squalor.

As he sat down in the chair the old guy passed me a kitchen tea towel that was full of tea stains, but seeing as I had no other towel with me I had no choice but to use it. Whilst cutting his hair he started telling me how his wife was in hospital with Alzheimer's and that his son lived so far away he couldn't visit him much. He could have been filling me with a pack of lies but being a trusting person I slowly found myself feeling sorry for him. He got up in the middle of me trying to cut his hair and trotted off to the living room; he brought back a children's colouring book to show me.

'This is what I do with my time' he said as he started flicking through the pages that had been coloured in.

After I had cut his hair he ask me to stay and have a cup of tea with him. There was no way I was going to drink tea from that kitchen, but so as not to hurt his feelings I agreed.

'Yes that would be nice'

The cups he was using were so dirty but I had no option other than to take it from him. He talked more about his wife and son and slowly I found myself telling him that I was married with a child and so on….. then just as I was about to get up he said.

'Russell, I can see that you're a kind fellow and was wondering if you could do something for me before you leave?'

'Yes, what is it?'

'I find it so hard getting up and down the stairs and this makes it hard for me to have a bath. Is it possible that you could run the bath for me and help me in, you see I can't get in and out of it on my own'.

I just stood there staring at him. Did I hear him right? Me help him in the bath! He must have seen my face change because before I could answer he said.

'I'm sorry, I shouldn't have asked you to do that. Come on, I'll show you out. I'm sorry'.

As a feeling of pity took over me I found myself saying.

'No no, don't worry. Yes of course I'll help you'

'The bathroom is just at the top of the stairs, by the time you have run the bath I should have made it up there'

'Do you want me to help you up the stairs?'

'No thanks lad, you go on up, by the time you've run the bath I'll be up there'

As I started to climb the stairs I couldn't believe how dirty they were. They looked like they hadn't seen a hoover for years. Even though the downstairs of the house should have prepared me, I still couldn't believe my eyes when I got into the bathroom. I could barely see the bottom of the bath through all the cobwebs and I don't know how many huge black spiders there were. This was the icing on the cake for someone who has arachnophobia! I stood there thinking 'Oh shit' I hate bleeding spiders but in the background I could hear the old guy trying to get up the stairs, puffing and panting on his way. I started running the water and trying to clean away the cobwebs without touching the spiders. I looked around for something to use, anything, but in the end I had no choice other than to use my hands. There was nothing in this bathroom, not even a bar of soap.

The bath started to fill up with water but there was no plug in it. I watched all the spiders frantically 'paddling' their legs, fighting for their lives and all the time their bleeding cobwebs were blocking the plug hole.

'Shit, shit' I thought.

Time was running out before he reached the bathroom and I didn't want him to feel embarrassed. In an act of desperation I stuck my finger in the plug hole and began pushing the spiders and their cobwebs down the plug hole. It felt like it was taking for ever but I finally did it. By the time the bath was full, true to his word he had made it up the stairs. As I turned around I saw this man who must have been eighty or more stood naked holding on to the door frame, shaking with cold.

'It won't be a minute'

'OK lad, don't worry'

'Do you have any towels?'

' I think there should be some in the airing cupboard over there' he said pointing to the other side of the hall.

As I passed him I was thinking shit, you watch something jump out of the cupboard at me now. I found a towel and after turning the water off I helped him in the bath.

'If you don't mind waiting on the landing lad I wont be long' he said

Waiting? Why, I thought I'm off, but then I realised I couldn't leave him there unable to get out. I couldn't believe the situation I had got myself into, and thought nobody will ever believe this.
When he was ready I helped him out of the bath and back down the stairs. He seemed so grateful, and as I was leaving he gave me his

colouring book and some crayons and said 'please give this to your daughter from me'. I took the book and left. When I eventually got home I gave the book and crayons to my daughter and went into the other room to tell my wife why I was late and what had just happened. As I was telling my wife the story, my daughter came into the room crying.

'What's wrong babe, why are you crying?'

'Because you've coloured all the pages in.'

My wife and I just laughed but as I was doing so remembered I hadn't even charged him the £2.50 fee. Not so funny now I thought! The next day the staff at work laughed at me when I told them what had gone on. I wondered if he would have asked any of the girls to do the same if they had gone around to his house. I like to think he wouldn't have.

A few weeks later he telephoned the salon again for his hair cut, or was it a bath we all thought? I didn't go but I asked one of the clients who worked for home help to visit him and see if he was OK.

Sometimes it is hard not to get involved with your clients even though some of them like to consider you as much more than just a hairdresser.
One particular client forgot that I was just her hairdresser and needed much more help than I could ever have offered her.

Jackie was a lovely girl who lived at home with her mother, and like most young girls was keen to find herself a boyfriend as soon as she could. She was one of those clients who, if I saw her out socially, would take it upon herself to come over and join in the conversation with whoever I was with. If she was passing the salon she would call in for a quick chat regardless of whether she had a hair appointment or not.

It wasn't long before she found herself a boyfriend and got pregnant. Before they had even had chance to move in together Jackie's boyfriend found himself in trouble with the law, which resulted in him going to prison before the baby was born. This obviously came as a bit of a blow for Jackie, especially with a new baby on the way, however she set about finding a home in readiness for him being released. On the day of his release Jackie and her mother went to pick him up and take him to their new home, and for a while things seemed to go OK. Jackie would call in the salon with her new baby and tell us how well she and her boyfriend were getting on with each other and with parenthood. Jackie was my last client one Saturday night and was having her hair done to go out on her first night out since having the baby while her boyfriend was staying in to baby-sit. From what I was told the story goes like this;

When Jackie got home from her night out she was horrified to find her baby dead in its bed. Screaming, she ran into the bedroom in which her boyfriend was asleep. When the emergency services arrived they at first thought it was a cot death. The new baby and some of its possessions were taken away from the home. Following a post mortem it was revealed that the child had been shaken so much it had suffered a brain hemorrhage and consequently her boyfriend was arrested. Poor Jackie went back to live with her mother and of course the boyfriend went back to prison but this time for a very long stretch. Understandably Jackie was upset, hurt and very lonely and although she had many friends she could talk to, she seemed to keep them at a distance. Maybe sometimes it's better to talk to strangers instead of your close friends, and at this time Jackie decided to confide in me.

She would call into the salon every day wanting to talk; sometimes she would wait around for hours just so she could sit for ten minutes with me. It was so sad to see this girl who had lost everything, her child, boyfriend, home and job. She just wanted me to sit and listen to her all day, but being in work it was difficult to meet this kind of need. I did try, but there wasn't a lot I could do or say. Sometimes I found myself scared of saying anything to her in case it was the wrong thing to say. After a few weeks my boss came up to me and told me I had to stop Jackie calling in the salon all the time.

As sad as it was, I knew he was right, and we felt it wasn't doing Jackie any good. I had to go and see her and her mother at their home and explain what my boss had said. She did stop coming into the salon but instead started to phone up, pleading with the staff to get me to the phone. Again I was told I couldn't keep the phone line busy for such long periods of time, and eventually her communication with me and the salon ceased. I believe Jackie and her mother moved away to be closer to Jackie's mother's family. The whole situation was so so sad, but Jackie needed much more help then I could ever have offered her, and the right help.

The most bizarre thing I was ever asked to do happened when I was living in Manchester. I had been doing the hair of one particular family for some years when suddenly the husband died, so the salon sent the family a bereavement card as we often did. A few days later I was asked to go to reception because there was someone there to see me. I got there to find the bereaved wife and daughter stood waiting for me. After saying how sorry I was to hear about their loss the daughter said

'We want to know if you could do something for us please. Well for dad?'.

'Yes, if I can'

'Me and mum wanted to do one last thing for dad'

'OK, what is it you want to do?'

'Daddy's coming home tomorrow to spend his last night at home before his funeral and we would be very grateful if you would call around and cut his hair'

'It's the last thing we can do for daddy' said the daughter.

I couldn't believe what they were asking me to do! I just stood there looking at them.

'Oh please' said the daughter 'it's the last thing we can do for him'

I felt like saying well you fucking cut it then but of course didn't. I understood they were grieving but I had to say no.

They never came back in the salon for their hair cut from that day on. A year later I heard that the wife had died, but I knew that had I cut the husband's hair when he died there would have been an expectation for me to do the mother's hair. I'm so glad there are people that are able to do this kind of work, but I find it hard enough working on the living, I wasn't going to shit myself working on the dead as well.

A few years ago, well before I opened my salon in North Wales, I was asked if I'd go around to a lady's house and cut her hair. I had never spoken to this lady but knew of her and from what I'd been told she was very fond of a tipple or two. Apart from this, the only other thing I'd been told was that she lived with her two young children and that she and her partner had split up. I was the hairdresser of quite a few of her friends and colleagues and therefore assumed she knew I was gay.

I arrived at her glass front door and shortly after ringing the door bell I saw a figure coming down the stairs in what looked like a yellow dressing gown. She opened the door and we both said a quick hello as I walked into the hallway. Just as I turned around to ask which room she would like me to go into she pushed me up against the wall. I stood there frozen, still holding onto my bags which were full of all my hairdressing tools. Suddenly her face came right up to mine and she started kissing me full on. Immediately I could smell the drink on her breath and from the force of her hold knew I wasn't going to get out of this situation easily.

My mind was running wild, trying to think what I could do to escape her. To buy me some time I dropped the bags I was holding and took hold of her. I turned her around and started to kiss her back but how my legs held me up I've no idea. Her hands started to roam all over me so eagerly you'd have swore she had ten pairs of hands. Pulling away I gave her one more kiss before I asked

'Can I use your bathroom?'

'Yes sure, would you like me to make you a drink for when you come down?'

'Yes please' I said 'That would be good'

I could tell she thought she was going to get lucky that night! After locking myself in her bathroom I was walking around like a headless chicken thinking shit, shit what am I going to do? Then I remembered I had my mobile phone with me. Thank god for mobile phones, if this had been a few years earlier before mobile phones were out I dread to think what might have happened.

'Tommy, Tommy' I said to my brother in a low voice.

'Please call me back in two minutes'

'Why what's wrong?' he said 'and why are you talking in a low voice ?'

'I'll tell you later just please, please don't forget to call me'

I wanted her to believe that whatever she thought she was going to get that night that I was well up for it too. I walked over to her trying to look as straight and butch as possible but really I wanted to be sick with fear. She handed me my drink and I downed it in one (to this day I still have no idea what the hell it was I drank). Putting my glass down I took hold of her and began kissing her the best way I new how and once again her bloody hands sprang straight back in action. All the time I was thinking come on phone, fucking ring. It seemed like forever but in the end it did. Pulling away I said

'I'm so sorry I'll have to take this call, my father isn't very well'

Poor dad, he was as fit as a fiddle, but I had to say something.

I stayed on the phone for the rest of the time I was there.

'Oh my God, thanks for calling Tommy, I'm on my way'

Putting my hand over the phone I said.

'I'm so sorry I have to go, but what are the chances of me calling back later? Will you still be up?'

'Yeah you have my number call me, I'm in all night'

Grabbing my hairdressing things I could hear my brother shouting down the phone. 'What the fuck's going on?'

'I'm coming now Tom, just wait one minute'

Stepping out of her front door I turned around and pulling a sad face I said

'I'm so sorry but I'll see you later'

'OK, I'll be waiting'

Smiling back I thought, you'll be waiting a long fucking time.

My poor brother was still shouting down the phone as I walked off. Looking back it seems so funny now but at the time I hated it. When I told my brother what had just happened he said

'Get the fuck back in there. If she wants to sort you out then let her, I'd never walk away from that'

But that's typical coming from a straight guy. No amount of money would have got me back into that house. She did call me a few times afterwards but I always told her I was busy.

My experience with this next client was very different to any other mobile visit I'd ever made. Fay's mother called to my house one day and asked if I would go around to cut her daughter's hair. I had never seen Fay but knew she was in a wheel chair because she had been in some kind of accident when she was younger. Walking up the ramp to Fay's house I had no idea what to expect or what she would want doing with hair. I wandered whether her hair would have already be washed and if not, would I be able to wash it because of the wheel chair access? How old was she? Could she look after her hair herself? Just then the door opened.

'Thanks for coming Russell' said Fay's mother

'They always say they'll come (Mobile Hairdressers) but when they know Fay's in a wheel chair they never turn up. They must think that it's too much trouble'

'Don't worry, has she had her hair washed or would you like me to do it for her?'

'No, I washed it just before you came. Come on in, Fay's in here, this is her own living area and anything you want you'll find in here'

As we walked in I could see that Fay was sat looking out of the window with her back to us. Looking at the back of her hair I could see it was very long and dark.

'Fay, Russell's here to do your hair love'

Fay couldn't turn around very well in her wheelchair because she had difficulty moving her hands. As Fay's mother wheeled her around I got my first look at Fay's hair and face. She must have been twenty seven or twenty eight, a good ten years older than me.

'Hello' she said 'Thank you so much for coming'

'Oh that's OK' I said 'but by the way your hair looks I don't think you need me. You have beautiful hair'

'I'll leave you both to it' said Fays mother 'and if there is anything you want, either of you, just give me a shout, I'm only down the hall'

'Okay mum' said Fay. 'Thanks for saying that Russell, but I think it's getting a little long now. I'd just like an inch or two off'

Fay was one of the easiest mobile clients I could have had; her hair was already washed when I got there and all I had to do was trim it and blow dry it. I thought the other hairdressers were mad never to come back and do her hair again. I found Fay very friendly and very chatty, and sometimes very frank. I must have done Fay's hair a few times when one day she asked

'Are you still a virgin?'

'Err yes' I replied, feeling very embarrassed.

You'll Never Make a Hairdresser

'Do you have any pubic hair yet?' she enquired further.

'Yes, why?' I asked back.

'Oh, just wondering'

I wanted to finish her hair quickly that day and leave because she was starting to make me feel uneasy when suddenly she announced

'You can fuck me if you want to'

'What?' I said

'You heard me. When you've done my hair you can do it to me but you'll have to hurry up because my mother will be back soon from shopping'

Only moments ago I had wanted to do this cut and blow as quick as I could to escape the conversation, and now I wanted it to last forever in order to delay the inevitable or to buy enough time for her mother to return!

'That will do thanks. Now go over and lock the door' she instructed.

I felt like I was walking in slow motion; I could see the door but it never seemed to get any nearer.

'Come on, we've got to be quick'

After locking the door I turned around to hear her say.

'Come closer, come on. Now pull you pants down'

To this day I will never know why I did what I was told to do. Was it because she was a lot older than me and I felt at the time I had to do what I was told, or at the back of my mind did I really want to do it? Maybe I'll never know the answer. With the hand that had some movement she tried to take hold of me. At the time I didn't know whether I was feeling joy or pain, and I wanted to scream 'stop' at her and run as fast as I could from that house; but a part of me also wanted to stay. I just stood there and allowed her to touch and domineer me, yet I was the one who if I wanted to could walk away.

'Now take them off, and pull down my knickers'

'but'

'come on, it's OK'

As I started to lift her skirt I remember feeling so scared. Scared of not knowing what I was going to find underneath, so I turned my head away as I pulled and twisted on her knickers. I didn't want to take them down, nor did I want to be on my knees in front of Fay pulling at her knickers, almost dragging at them. Finally they came free.

'Put them under my pillow; I don't want my mother to find them left lying around.'

'I think I should go' I said slipping her knickers under her pillow 'I don't know what I'm doing. I think I'll get dressed and go.'

'No, come over here, please, you can't go now.'

'Fay, I've never'

Before I could finish what I was saying she said

'It doesn't matter, just put it in here'

'Whatttt?'

'Just do it' she insisted, after which she went silent.

My whole body felt hot, I couldn't believe what was happening but I knew by this time I didn't want it to stop. Just when I thought my heart was going to burst out of my chest she pulled away and said.

'Now you can put it in there'

Looking down all I could see was hair which almost made me ask where? I decided to just go for it. As I got closer Fay put her head back and closed her eyes. God job because she would of thought I looked like Houdini the position I had to get in.

'Now push slowly' she said

Just as I started to push her wheel chair moved backwards.

'Put the brake on and do it again'

After pulling on the brake I finally got myself back into position and began to push once more. Fay's head shot back and still with her eyes closed she started to moan. Again the wheel chair started to move around slowly because in all the commotion I'd only put the brake on at one side. Still pushing I was trying franticly to grab the other brake but there was no way I could reach it from where I was.

I didn't like what I was doing, never mind what I was feeling and as I looked down I couldn't even see the other part of my body but I knew the sensation I was getting was not nice. By this time Fay had started to look more like something out of the exorcist, throwing her head around and making silly noises. My hands held on to the wheel chair for dear life and my back felt as if it was going to snap at any minute; my knees were bent and my toes were killing me because they were constantly trying to keep up with the pace at which me and the wheel chair were moving around the room in one big continual circle.

I caught sight of all this in the large mirror on the wall and thought I looked more like a crab the way I was bent down, legs going ten to the dozen, running around after the wheel chair. Pulling myself up I said

'I have to go.'

'No please, please stay, come on that was nice.'

'No I'm sorry I have to go. I've got to get home.'

'Did you like that?'

From the way Fay was smiling I knew that she had.

'Yes it was good.'

'We'll do it again then?'

'Yeah sure we will.'

My back was still killing me as I bent down and started to pull my pants on and all the time I was thinking never in my life will I do that again. Now I knew why all the other hairdressers had never returned. That night I told my brother Tommy all about it and all he could ask was 'Did she have nice tits?' He laughed when I said 'I have no idea, with all what was going on I had no time for tits an all' That was the last time I saw Fay and every time her mother called to ask if I could do Fay's hair I told her I was busy.

Looking back now it's mad how I allowed the whole thing to happen, but it also makes me remember how naive I was. More importantly though it reminds us that just because Fay had a disability and was in a wheelchair she still had the same need for a sex life as any able bodied person, and good luck to her I say as long as I didn't have to do all that again.

You'll Never Make a Hairdresser

Salon clients

Johnny often laughs and says my salon should be called the boardroom, the reason being there are so many stories told and decisions made there and usually no one knows what the hell they are talking about. He is right sometimes!

A lot of clients will absorb any information given to them by their hairdresser without ever questioning the validity of what they're being told. Whether commenting on local gossip, the quality of food in a local restaurant or the standard of a holiday resort, hairdressers are a great source of information. Whether this is based on fact or fiction really doesn't matter, hairdressers will always have been fed enough information to pass on from one client to the next. For example, if I to was opening a bar or restaurant the first thing I would do before opening would be to invite local businesses in for some free food or drinks. Word of mouth is the best way of advertising locally and this free hospitality would be a sure way of getting the customers in, especially if the local hairdressers were on the guest list.

People talk to their hairdressers all the time, and equally salon stylists never stop talking all day. They will often past on all the information they have learned that day to their next client, and the next, and so on, whether this information is correct or not.

If you ask your stylist how the new bar is up the road, even if they have never been there they will tell you about someone who has, and what they thought of it, regardless of whether it is good or bad information that is being passed on. I've seen it happen so many times. So if anyone is thinking of starting their own business think of all the places that for the price of a meal or a free drink you could get really good, free advertising from. If you believe you have something good to offer why not let others shout out about how good you are. In my salon all I ever ask of my staff is that they don't comment on something until they have experienced it themselves. After all, passing on inaccurate information can be counter effective on the business that they depend on for their own wage each week.

When I first opened my salon in Prestatyn I already had a good clientele but most of my stylists didn't. As part of my setting up cost for the new salon I incorporated the wages for all the staff for that first week. I made sure that we were all kept busy in our first week and it was my intention that the salon wouldn't make one penny in that first week!

'What's it going to be? When are you opening? What's your telephone number?' people were asking as they popped their head around the door to watch us put the finishing touches to the décor.

Rather than booking any appointments for paying customers that week we just handed out our business cards and explained that the first week was already fully booked. Each stylist was given a full quota of free cuts for their family and friends and were all paid regardless. So, a new salon in town which was already fully booked for its first week must be a good one! The investment of a week's wages for each of the staff was well worth it.

Every time a passer by looked in during our first week of opening the shop floor was packed. This had the desired effect, and within no time the following weeks and months were booked up with new paying customers. On top of everything else this gave our new team a good opportunity for a week's training, and for the team to build a good rapport with each other. The Tuesday morning on which we opened the salon it was buzzing, people calling in with flowers, cards and messages of good luck, and others wanting their hair done there and then. Sorry, we'd say, but we don't have anything until a week today and so they would book in. Word soon got around that there was quite a waiting list.

Every day in a hairdressing salon is so different from the day before. Each time you walk up to your next client, unless they are one of your regulars you never quite know what they are going to say or what they will want to talk about. Each stylist is usually stood with a client for up to an hour at a time, or on occasions up to three hours, depending on what the customer is having done. It is the responsibility of the stylist to make the customer feel at ease and to pitch the conversation at the right level. This can be a difficult task when you are faced with someone who for no particular reason you have taken a dislike to, just like you it happens to hairdressers too.

The first task the stylist has is to gather as much information about his or her client as quickly as possible. Not only does this break the ice but it also forms a foundation to build the rest of the conversation on. When a stylist walks towards you they will instantly make an assumption about you and this is usually based on the way you are dressed. Once you start to talk the stylist can usually determine whether your clothes suit your personality or whether you have just got dressed up to come into the salon. Believe me, it all helps us, and usually by the time you are gowned and seated we have got you off to a tee within minutes.

We will always try to say a quick hello to a client before they are seated. Just a quick exchange of words will usually determine where in the salon we will seat that particular client. For instance if someone came into the salon saying

'Oh my god it's pissing down out there'

for all she may be the nicest person in the world she wouldn't be seated
next to the actress or MP who is having a colour. They would be seated on the other side of the salon where they can entertain the staff to their heart's content without causing offence to others and without the salon losing any of its more refined clientele.
This in itself can be quite funny when you have to flit from one client to the other, especially as you have to change your mindset and tone of conversation between each of them.

You find yourself talking to one person about how nice her ring is that her husband has just bought her and how he paid twenty thousand pounds for it. Then you go over the other side of the salon to where your next client will tell you how she's been putting a pound a week away just so she could come to your salon to have her hair done. It's not easy to do, but believe me If I had the choice I'd be more at home talking to the pound a week client and we'd also have a great laugh too.

With a regular client you can miss out on all the niceties such as where they live, the weather and their next holiday and you can usually pick up from where you last left off. With a new client it's harder to establish that comfort zone. First we start with the weather or holidays and if that comes to a quick end we move on to

'Do you live around here?'

'Have you been here before?'

'Where do you normally go for your hair cut?'

'Are you working at the moment?'

If this fails and the client still won't engage in conversation then the rest of the appointment is carried out in silence with the exception of some crucial questions about the cut or style. It's sometimes nice when this does happen as it can be really exhausting talking constant crap for ten hours a day!!

I once went up to a client and after we had decided on what she was having done that day I asked her.

'Are you going out tonight?'

'You can cut the crap out love and just do my hair' she rudely replied!

I was dying to laugh. It was not as if I'd really wanted to talk her anyway. But seeing she'd asked in such a nasty way I obliged, and for once in my hairdressing life I did slip the word crap into my cut. She never came back again!!

I had a client one day who was wearing a patch over one of her eyes and as sad as it was that she had to wear this patch she refused to take it off while I cut her hair. The band holding the patch on was going right around the back of her head. She had asked for a bob hair cut which involves combing the hair right into the nape of the neck to do the first cut, then following the same process with each new section. I explained I could not guarantee she would get the best hair cut if she insisted that the patch had to stay on. To try and reach a compromise I asked if she would just hold the patch over her eye while I did my cut.

'No' she retorted in a nasty voice and then asked

'Just how long have you been hairdressing?'

You'll Never Make a Hairdresser

'I've been hairdressing for over twenty years' I replied then I asked.

'Would you mind if I asked what you do for a living?'

With a look that could kill she said

'I work for a dry cleaning company, why?'

'Have you ever been asked to iron a shirt while your client is still wearing it?' I asked, making my point.

As I took hold of her gown I handed it to one of my staff and instructed them to see her out.

'You can't do that. I want to speak to the salon manager' she said.

'Lady' I said smiling 'I can do anything I wish, I am the salon manager'.

And another one bit the dust!!

Don't get me wrong, I love my job and on most occasions go far out of my way to help people if I can. But I will not take any shit that is fired my way and nor should any other hairdresser. Why should we? What I tell my stylist is 'Don't forget they have come to you, you have not gone out and dragged them in off the street'.

Hairdressers should always remember if there is any way that your client can help you to do a better job of their hair, then ask them to do it. If they know they will get a better hair cut they will be more than willing to help. e.g. head down or if need be getting them to stand up. A lady came into the salon one day with hair right down past her waist and she only asked for an inch to be taken off.

'Would you be able to stand up for me?' I said.

'Why?' she asked 'Will I get a better hair cut?'

'Oh yes' I replied.

'And how's that?' she said.

'Because believe me' I said smiling. 'If I'm on my knees it will be the quickest hair cut you've ever had'.

With that she jumped up and never moved. Both of us were left happy. She got the better hair cut and I didn't have to kneel down.

I wish I had a pound for every client that has sat down and said

'I'm going out tonight and I want a new hair do, I'll leave it up to you what I have'.

This isn't so bad when you have been doing your client's hair for a long time and you have got to know the client and their life style and what they can and cannot do with their own hair. Maybe some hairdressers don't mind it, or maybe some may prefer it but I don't. I could scream.

You wouldn't walk into Next and stand at the desk while the assistant runs around the shop looking for a size 12 dress you can wear that night, or call the local take out and ask them to send over some food that they think you will like. So why would they want me to choose what they wear on their heads for the next six weeks? When I have, and no matter how many times I've shown them how to do it, they will call you a day or two later saying

'I can't do my hair'.

What a surprise! Then you have to do it all over again, only this time the way they say. You're left hoping you haven't cut too much off because after all you were given a free hand. We never charge them the second time but we should do, after all you could be doing a paying client's hair who knew what they wanted.

Whenever a stylist is busy with a client we always try not to disturb them. I am always being asked to go to the telephone and when I get there it is either a client wanting to book an appointment (why she didn't ask the receptionist to do this I don't know) or it's some sales person on the other side of the world trying to sell me house insurance. It's so annoying.

Not too long ago I was cutting away when one of my staff came up to me and said I was wanted in the reception.

You'll Never Make a Hairdresser

'I'm so sorry' I said to my client. 'I'll be back in a minute'.

Luckily this client didn't mind. Once I got to the reception I noticed a lady whose hair I had cut earlier that day. Because I was told by the receptionist that this lady would not go away until I had come to see her, I was sure she was going to tell me she wasn't happy with her hair.

As I got closer to her she pulled a dress out of her bag and said.

'Russell, as you know my boyfriend is taking me out tonight and I wanted to know if you think this dress will suit me?
If you don't the lady in the shop said I could take it back!'.

I just stood there in shock, then she said

'Would you like me to try it on?'

'Oh no' I said.

Apart from being shocked I was also angry that this lady had made me leave a paying client to come all the way down to reception just to look at her dress. She had had her hair done that day uninterrupted and I'm sure she wouldn't have liked it if she had been left sat in my chair with wet hair while some woman came to show me her dress. I didn't not know what to say about the dress, but I knew I would never have worn it!

'It's very nice' I said. 'Very nice. I'm sure he'll love it'.

I didn't have the heart to say I had just done her boyfriend's hair and he was planning to end their relationship that night. Well it wasn't for me to say, new dress or not!
As I have said before it's sometimes hard not to get involved with your clients especially when you have been doing their hair for a number of years.

I had been doing Jean's hair for a long time and she was one of those clients that I also looked forward to doing. She was so gentle and so caring towards other people and such a good mother and wife. I knew she had been married for many years and her children were growing up fast. Like all mothers she adored her children. She and her husband had good jobs which helped pay for the beautiful house they lived in.

I remember thinking how strange it was that she never ever mentioned her husband, but always talked about her children. Then one day she came into the salon for her usual appointment with a black eye. She had hit her head on the kitchen cupboard. Months later she arrived with her hand in plaster. She had fallen outside her house. Three months later she had stitches in the back of her head, she had hit her head on the garage door.
I could tell this particular day she looked so sad, or maybe she felt embarrassed because I said.

'You should be more careful, there is always something happening to you'.

Then I remembered all the other times she had come into the salon with something wrong with her. I gave her my home telephone number and told her if she ever needed me for anything she knew where I was. I knew she understood me by the way she looked at me. I also knew all the things that she said were happening to her were not accidents. I didn't want to embarrasses her by telling her my thoughts; I just wanted her to know I was there.

Then one day I was called to the salon phone and it was Jean's husband.

'Jean will not be coming this week Russell, she's had a bump in her car'.

He told me that she was going to be OK and thankfully there was no one else in the car with her. I was shocked and offered to call around to their house for Jean to have her hair washed and blown.

'No' he said. 'she's in a wheel chair with a broken leg, she'll be in touch with you soon'.

I knew he had done it, but what could I do? I knew if I'd had called anyone it wouldn't have done her any good and I knew she would never leave him. When Jean came into the salon for her next appointment I saw her being pushed in the wheel chair by her husband. I couldn't believe it. I felt so sorry for her and could sense by the way she and her husband were talking she just wanted him to leave.

When doing her hair she told me about the accident she and her husband had had in his car. I knew then that he was the one that had done this and all the other things that had been wrong with Jean in the past. Jeans husband told me she was the only one in the car, her car. This beautiful lady was so caring to everyone she came into contact with, loved her family so much and was still being loyal to the man she married. Why?.

She knew that I knew what was going on. We never talked about it but she knew if she ever wanted any help she could call me any time. I wanted to tell someone but I didn't want to lose her as a client; not because of the weekly money she brought into the salon, but because I still wanted to see her, to know that she was OK. I knew she wasn't ready to ask for my help yet.

A male customer once visited a salon I worked at in Torquay. On this particular day I was taking charge of the salon whilst the owner was off on leave. It was a reasonably large salon and was busy with clients and staff. I was approached by one of the female stylists who insisted that she needed help with a customer who had just come in for a dry hair cut. As we walked over to the man who was in his late forties to early fifties noticed he was gowned and sat in front of the mirror smiling. The stylist explained that he was fondling himself under the cutting gown and that she found this behaviour unacceptable. I immediately looked down at the gown only to see it frantically moving up and down. Without hesitation I leant over and undid his gown. 'Leave now you dirty bastard' I said in both shock and anger.

I have never wanted the ground to open up so much in my life as when the man explained that he suffered from Parkinson's. Despite apologising the customer refused to stay. Never have I felt so guilty about jumping to such an inaccurate conclusion. But it just goes to show that you never know what you're going to be faced with!

Sex in the salon

What is it about straight women and gay men? Or come to that gay men and straight women? When ever you meet a gay man you can bet his best friend is a straight woman. Doesn't every straight woman have a least one gay friend? It makes me smile when a woman knows you're gay and says

'Oh I have a friend that's gay'

It's as if we're the ultimate fashion accessory for many of the straight women out there; I believe we're the next best thing to a Chanel bag. And hasn't every gay man had a straight woman come on to him at least once in his life time? I know I have. Why do they do this? Do they honestly believe that if they could get a gay man into bed for just one night, then he would wake up and no longer be gay? (I don't think so!) It always makes me laugh when I hear a straight woman say

'Why are all the handsome men gay?'

Sure, there are some very handsome gay men out there, but you ask any gay man and he'll tell you just how many handsome straight guys there are too. I've heard it said that the difference between a gay man and a straight man is two pints of lager; if only that were true.

A lady very well respected in the community came into the salon one day. She was married to a very nice man and had two beautiful children. I do the hair for the whole family and have got to know them all very well over the years. I don't know if the lady was trying to shock me but when ever she came into the salon alone for her hair cut she would always talk about sex.
A lot of clients talk about sex, I just carry on working and listen, but when this lady talked about it she would go beyond what many would call acceptable; the words she chose to use often offended even a broad minded man like me!

'How are you today' I'd say.

'Oh fine love, I've not been out of bed long. It's my husband, he just

You'll Never Make a Hairdresser

loves fucking me. Even at his age'.

Sometimes I'd think to myself have I heard her right?

'Oh your arse looks so fucking hot in those pants today' she'd say.

Once she even said. 'If I put your hand up my skirt do you think you'll like it?'

'I can assure you I won't' I said.

'Why don't you come in there with me (pointing to the stock cupboard)and I'll show you all my naughty bits' The list is endless.

She was getting that bad I wouldn't cut her hair unless another member of staff agreed to stand with me. They would have to pretend they were watching what cut I was doing. On these occasions she would say little bits but was never as bad. I often thought why? Why did she do this? I don't think she was as happy as she was making out she was.

Was she always having sex with her husband? I doubt it very much, and if she was I didn't want to know. Maybe her husband was having all this sex but you can bet it wasn't with her. To look at her you would never believe she would talk or act in this way. Maybe it all comes back to that old saying 'fur coat and no kickers'.

'Mrs Hughes is on the phone' the receptionist said.

'The Mrs Hughes?' I would say back to the receptionist.

There is only one Mrs Hughes and no one in the salon liked doing her hair. I myself have never done her hair and never will. I believe if there is ever anyone that is, shall we say 'not all there' then it's Mrs Hughes. The salon was full this particular day when Mrs Hughes walked in.

After being gowned and seated Mrs Hughes started telling her stylist what she wanted to be done with her hair that day. I don't know how or why but somehow their conversation got on to me.

'I think Russell is really nice, is he seeing anyone?' asked Mrs Hughes.

'Yes' my stylist replied. 'He's married to Jonathan'.

'Jonathan !' she said. 'I didn't know he was gay'.

With that Mrs Hughes got up and walked over to the other side of the salon where I was working on a very nice lady who was also a new client. When Mrs Hughes came over to me she said in a very loud voice so all the salon could hear.

'I didn't know you sucked cock'.

I couldn't believe what she had just said. Everyone in the salon turned around and stared at her then at me.

'Well' said Mrs Hughes, still standing next to me and obviously still waiting for an reply.

'When I can' I said. 'When I can'.

The whole salon fell about laughing and then the situation was quickly defused.

There are many clients that I am happy to share my personal life with, but there are also clients that I would prefer not to share things with. On this day I had no choice but to come back with something witty.

On another occasion the same Mrs Hughes walked into the salon and I was the only stylist working on the shop floor. Her stylist came out from the staff room and I could hear them discussing what hair colour she was going to have that day. I took the time to apologise beforehand to my client for what Mrs Hughes might or might not say. I was so glad I had.

'It's OK love' said my client 'I've lived in Liverpool for the past twenty years; there aren't many things that would offend me'

As Mrs Hughes' stylist walked off to mix her colour Mrs Hughes turned around to me and my client and said

'I'm sorry I'm late but it's because of my boyfriend. He said he had to have a wank before he brought me. Do you watch porn Russell when you wank? He has to all the time.'

I could feel my whole body shaking with anger and embarrassment.

'Excuse me' I said to my client as I rushed off into the staff room.

'Get that fucking woman out of my salon now'

'I've just mixed her hair colour' said the stylist.

'I don't give a shit what you've mixed, get her out of here now'.

With that I went back to my own client and apologised again. Liverpool or not I could tell she had been offended by what Mrs Hughes had said and who could blame her?. After doing my client's hair for all she loved it she never came back into the salon again. I wonder why?

Some of the staff found it funny but it was far from funny to me. When I got home and told Johnny what had happened he asked

'Well did you answer her?'

'No I fucking didn't' I said. 'I believe that some questions should remain unanswered'.

After doing a lady's hair I stood talking to her in the reception area while she waited for her husband to pick her up. When her husband arrived my client introduced me to him then they both left. It is always nice to be able to meet their husbands, and it's good to put a face to a name.

A few nights later I was in the salon alone when I saw this guy coming out of the pub that faces the salon. He saw me and started walking over, I could see it was my client's husband. As he walked into the salon I said, 'Hello, how are you?'

'I'm fine thank you, and you?'

'I've finished for the day now, just a few things to put away them I'm off home'.

I could see that he'd been drinking.

'Been watching you from the pub and could see that you were alone, I wanted to tell you something'

'What?' I said feeling very uneasy.

'I'm a try sexual'

I didn't understand what he was going on about and neither did I like the way he was looking at me.

'What do you mean a try sexual?' I said.

'I'm willing to try anything' he said smiling.

To say I felt scared would be an understatement. I didn't know what this guy was capable of but I was not going to allow him to enter my salon and make me feel the way I was feeling.

'I'm very happy for you' I said 'but if you don't get the fuck out of this shop I'm going to phone your wife'

With that said I walked over to the salon door and held it open for him to walk out, and walk out he did thank God. I believe he'd drank more than a few pints of lager but it just goes to show that after a few drinks there are straight men who are as he would put it a 'try sexual,' meaning they would try anything. I never told his wife but whenever she talks about him, I always think of him in quite a different light. He never did call to the salon to pick his wife up again.

I'd been doing this particular client's hair for some time when she asked if I would like to go out with her one night for a drink.
'Thank you very much,' I said 'but I'm seeing someone'
I didn't tell her I was gay and felt I didn't have to. It was my

You'll Never Make a Hairdresser

business and although I'm not ashamed of who finds out I feel I do not have to explain my life to all and sundry. She went on to say how sorry she was for asking me out when I was with someone else. I explained that she wasn't to know, and that we would just forget it.

After about six months she asked if I was still happy with my partner and I assured her I was. Some time later she came into the salon one Friday night when I was working late. There was only myself and one other stylist working that night and we were both in different rooms. She started telling me again how unhappy she was with her husband and how lonely she felt. I did feel sorry for her but at no time did I lead her on. After doing her hair I started walking out the room and towards the reception area.

'I'll be with you in a minute' she shouted getting her things together.

When she came to the reception I began to take her bill when she said in a low voice.

'I've left you a little something in the other room'

'Thank you very much' I said thinking it would be a tip.

We booked her next appointment and she left.
Before I could get though to the other room I heard the stylist shouting.

'Oh my god'

'What?' I asked entering the room.

'Look' She said pointing to the chair where I had just been cut the last lady's hair.

There on the chair were a pair of lady's knickers, and dirty knickers at that I might add. I couldn't believe it, and to say they were dirty is an understatement. We both laughed because we'd never seen anything like this in all our time in hairdressing. I got home and again told Johnny. He laughed but said I should have told her the first time she asked me to go out that I was gay. I still disagree; it's my life and I don't feel I have to tell every one whose hair I cut that

I am gay.

A few weeks later Johnny had a big meeting to go to and invited me along. I was just sitting there quietly when this woman walked in.

'Oh no' I said.

'What's wrong Russell?' Johnny asked.

'Oh nothing' I said.

Johnny looked around and with a smile on his face he said

'That's your knicker lady isn't it?'

I didn't have to say anything. He knew she was the one and with that he got up to greet her. After they had been chatting awhile he said

'I'd like to introduce you to my partner Russell.'

The look on her face, I had never seen anything like it and if anything I felt sorry for her. She never did turn up for her next appointment. Bless.

Ellen was in her late sixties and her husband a little older and I'd been doing her hair for years. When she told me that she and her husband were getting divorced I was shocked, as they seemed such a lovely couple. She went on to tell me that she and her husband were no longer having sex. It turned out her husband was under the doctor because he could no longer get an erection. He was obviously very upset and the doctors were doing all they could to find out what was wrong with him. Ellen was more than upset. She couldn't believe that their sex life was over. I was shocked that they had been together all that time, they were getting on in life and did sex really matter that much? It must have to her. Shouldn't she have been standing by her husband whom she had loved all that time?. For all she knew he could be ill. I couldn't really comment on this with her because I knew she wouldn't like what I had to say, so best say nothing I thought.

You'll Never Make a Hairdresser

The next time Ellen came in I asked how things were with her husband and if a divorce was still on the cards.

'Oh yes' she said 'the house is up for sale'.

She had taken her husband to see a specialist who dealt with his type of complaint.

'They have told him to use a pump on his penis' she said, 'but he won't, so I've told him I'm off'.

All the time I was thinking why?

Did she not feel any love for her husband? I suppose not. It was just before Christmas when their house sold. She had found a smaller house for herself and her husband was going to go and live with their daughter until his health was better, then he would find somewhere else to live. Two days before the move Ellen came down stairs and found her husband dead in the chair. He had been there all night. I was so sad for him.

From the way she reacted you'd never have thought that anything was ever wrong with their marriage. When she came into the salon to have her hair done for his funeral she sat there crying the whole time telling me what a wonderful husband he was. I'm sure she'd forgotten what she'd been telling me.

I wasn't on my best behaviour that day and I didn't want to know what she was telling me. I'd listened and remembered quite a different story from the last time she was in having her hair done, and this time she was making me feel angry. After the funeral she went ahead with the sale of her house and moved into the smaller one. Within a year she had also had a heart attack and died. I know that she never got to meet another man for the nice cosy nights in that she had longed for. Oh well, what goes around comes around, or so they say.

A long time ago I was employed by a salon in Wythenshawe, Manchester. The lady who owned it was married to a man a lot older then herself. They seemed a nice couple; he was retired and Ann still worked in the salon. I had been there about three months when the Christmas night out was coming up and we were told that it was staff only. I remember we all went for a meal and then on to a night club in Manchester where some of Ann's lady friends joined us. We'd all been drinking and by now I was well pissed, but I quickly started to sober up when one of the her friends came up to me and asked

'What do you think of Ann?'

Ann was a very nice person but she was also a lot older than me and extremely large.

'She's really nice' I said politely.

'Good' replied her friend. 'Because she's going to fuck you later in the back of her car.'

I looked over to the other side of the room towards Ann who was standing alone smiling back at me. I don't think I even finished my drink. I left the club and got a cab home as quickly as I could; there was no way on this earth I was going to stay around to catch a lift off her, boss or no boss!

On the day I returned to work Ann called me into her office and asked why I'd left the club so soon without telling her or any of the staff.

'I didn't feel too well' I said. 'So I got a cab and went home'

'There's no way I'd leave him for you' she said unexpectedly.

'Who?' I asked.

'My husband' she hissed in a nasty voice. 'I know you fancy me but I'm sorry it just wouldn't work out between us.'

I couldn't believe what she was saying. Me fancy her, was she going mad?

'I'd don't know who has told you that I fancy you Ann but I can assure you it's not true'

You'll Never Make a Hairdresser

'You're a liar. I can tell you like me'.

'How?' I asked.

'It's the way you look at me' she replied.
'I'm sorry Ann but if I wanted a woman I have a very beautiful wife at home and anyway your husbands got more chance of having me than you.' Whoops!

I must have hit a nerve because I was immediately sacked and told I must leave her salon. I was only in my twenties then and had no idea I could have probably had her done for sexual harassment. I don't even think I'd heard of sexual harassment back then. She thought she'd get her leg over on the staff night out and because I left early it all back fired. Thank God her friend had told me before I got into her car. I'm sure I wouldn't have got out alive if I had. Her weight alone would have killed me if she'd have pounced!

For the second time I went to work for my mother's friend Julie. She had asked me months earlier if I'd like to open a barber's section within her own salon which at the time only catered for ladies. Finding myself out of work I decide to say yes to the proposal. The room I was given had been used as a coat room for about fifteen years so let's just say it needed quite a bit of decorating to make it look anything like a barbers. That done, the barbers salon was ready for business. I was told I could only work on a self employed basis because Julie didn't have the money to employ me, but as the rent was set very low for the first six months all I had to do now was get the men in. At the time I opened the barbers I had been married for five years, my daughter was just starting school and life was going well. All I needed to do was make enough money to pay the shop rent and get some take home pay. Surely it couldn't be that hard, or could it?

The hours were so long. I've worked some hours in my time but these were the longest I'd ever worked and to say the barbers was small is surely the understatement of the year. There was just enough space for one cutting chair and the poor guys waiting for their hair cuts had to sit with their knees bent up on the low window sill that had been made into a make shift seat, their backs resting on the salon window (this would never be allowed today, what with all the health and safety regulations but needs must, as they say).

Julie must have been twenty years older than me if not more but I must admit she was one of the most beautiful women I had ever seen. I used to think she was so classy for her age (it just goes to show what a good dress and a bit of tanning cream can do for you). Over time we became very good friends, or so I thought.

Sometimes we would tell her husband and my wife that we had an appointment with our accountant, as a way of avoiding going straight home after work. Instead we'd go for a meal on a Friday night and just talk about work. It was all very harmless but wouldn't have looked right if our partners had found out.

The truth is we never discussed our home life much. We both knew the other was married and had a family and only the two of us knew just how hard the other worked to keep their family happy. So where was the harm in nipping out now and then for the odd meal? Occasionally she would say something that would make me think she was hitting on me, but because of our friendship I'd just laugh it off as a joke.

The barbers was slowly starting to build up trade but in between waiting for customers to come in I was starting to get bored. One day I was asked if I'd go in to the ladies salon because they were busy and there were two ladies wanting dry cuts. I put a sign on the barbers door and was off. The ladies loved their hair and asked if they could re-book with me. It didn't take long for me to get busy in the ladies salon as well, so between the two I was run off my feet all day every day. I was loving it but didn't see that behind the scenes the others weren't. My rent was now fixed at £70.00 pounds a week which was quite a lot of money twenty years ago, especially for an old cloak room.

It was agreed that I would get 40% of the money that I made from the ladies hair I did. Although I wasn't too happy with this there wasn't a lot I could do at the time. Every Saturday I would pay my rent at 4 O'clock. Because I had been busy with the ladies I would sometimes only have to pay ten or fifteen pounds because my 40% had off set the rest. By the end of the first month I was no longer paying rent and Julie was now paying me. Within six weeks I was rent free and getting a few hundred quid from Julie so what more could I ask for?

By now mine and Julie's friendship was full on. When I say this I mean there wasn't much we didn't do together; nights out, shopping, we even had a holiday with each other's family which if I'm honest I loved. I felt I could trust Julie with my life and that our friendship was for life.

Julie had some really nice friends; other business people, doctors, and those with the very funny hand shakes! So in time her nights out started to cost her more and more money. Money which had to be earned. The only problem was the clients she was earning her money from were slowly moving over to me. In one way she allowed it to happen. She had been happy for a while taking her 60% thinking I was the mug working for a 40% cut, so she could go off to spend the day with all her friends shaking hands backwards, sideways, upwards, downwards any fucking way as long as they didn't have to work. When she was in work all she talked about were the guys who had tried it on with her and who'd told her how nice she looked, not that I had that much time to listen. I had to get back to work to earn the money for her to go to all these dinners.

It wasn't long before our nights out stopped completely. She would storm around her own salon in a mood because I was so busy and half of the time she was taking my bills or cleaning the hair away while I moved on to my next client. Not very good when it's your own salon. She told me one day that she had no choice but to put my rent up again. This time it went up to one hundred pounds a week which was quite a jump, but I paid it. Little did she know I was making that in one day.

'I'm going away with the family,' she said one day. 'The only thing is I have no money. He thinks I've been making all this money but little does he know I've pissed it all up the wall'

'Don't cry Julie, we'll sort it out. I'll loan you some money' I offered.

'You will?'

'Yeah, how much do you need?'

'About a thousand pounds, you don't have that do you?'

'I'll get it, don't worry'

It was agreed that I'd keep all the money I earned the two weeks she was away with her family until I'd been paid back. Once I'd reached my one thousand pounds I would go back on the 40%. So as well as loaning her a thousand pounds I had to work like a dog to pay myself back. Something wasn't sounding right but what the hell, I did it and after all she might have been my boss but she was also my friend, right?

When Julie and her family arrived back from their holiday I had paid myself back and I had left two hundred and sixty pounds in the till for her. She was very pleased. She said she had been doing a lot of thinking and she had decided she could no longer keep up with the Joneses and would no longer keep trying. I was so glad my old Julie was back and she really began getting her head around her work again. Then one day he walked in.

He was the owner of a local shop that sold anything from bread to shoes. He was tall dark and very handsome. Because he was so handsome Julie did something that she had never done before and offered to help me out by cutting his hair. They seemed to get on well and this developed further over time. Our nights out to the accountants had just started up again when all of a sudden they stopped. Julie was having to go and see her accountant a lot more but now it Mr handsome who was with her. If Julie's husband should ever ring my house my wife was asked to say that I was out with Julie at the accountants. Which she did the few times he rang.

This would hopefully put him off the scent of what was really was going on. What she and I didn't think of at the time was that her husband would think that we were actually having an affair. It didn't cross my mind. I used to cut her husband's hair for him but this gradually stopped. I didn't mind as I never made any money cutting his hair anyway, and after all Julie was his wife. Things did seem odd when he started to behave a bit off with me. At first I just thought he was having a bad day but after a few months I thought there was more to it. I did mention this to Julie but she thought that he was getting a bit jealous that we were out so much.

'Me' I said 'I'm always at home. It's you that's always going out'. She just used to laugh it off.

The nights out didn't seem to be enough for Julie and Mr Handsome so they would go off in the day for hours on end. I'd find myself lying to both the staff and Julie's husband, always trying to cover up and make excuses for them. Because most of the time Julie's husband thought she was with me, looking back I can see now how it did look bad. However, because I knew I was always at work or home I never gave it that much thought at the time. To him though whenever she was out I was always with her. I suppose I should have known what was coming, but when he came into the salon one day like a raging bull I had no idea it was me he was coming for.

I should point out at this time that Julie's husband was one of the fattest men I had ever met and I always felt sorry for him when I'd hear Julie joking around telling people.

'Oh he thinks we have a great sex life, when really he's been fucking the crease of my leg for years' she'd laugh.

If I'm honest he might have been the fattest guy I'd met but he was one of the nicest men I knew.
He ran right up to me and grabbed hold of me. As he hit me in the face my whole body lifted up into the air and I landed on top of the draining board next to the sink. All the pots that had just been washed smashed as they went flying to the floor. (Not a nice place to land)

'I'll fucking kill you, sleeping with my wife' he ranted.

As I tried to get down (pots an' all) he came at me again. I didn't have time to tell him the truth before he hit me again, this time knocking me off the draining board. As I was sliding down the wall I could see his wife (my friend) in the background getting her bag and running out of the salon.

Thanks a fucking lot I was thinking, as I was getting myself ready for the next kicking he was about to give me. There was no way I could defend myself, for one I didn't have any time, and secondly I knew I would never stand a chance from the size of him alone. Best thing I thought was to wait until he'd had enough.

When he'd finished hitting me he dragged me out of the staff room right through the salon and threw me out of the salon door saying

'Don't fucking come back here again' (As if I ever would!)

Try going home and telling your wife that you've just had the shit kicked out of you for nothing, and lost your job at the same time because that's what had just happened. I rang the salon the next day to try and talk to Julie but all she said was she was so sorry. Her husband had got it into his head that we were having an affair. I never saw her again.

I thought it was nice of Mr Handsome to call to my house to see if I was OK. Maybe it was just his way of saying thanks for all the shit I had taken for him. Julie's husband used to drink in the same pub where my father drank. I say used to because when my father found out what he'd done to me he went up to him one night in the pub and smacked him right in the face saying 'That's off my son'. Thanks Dad.

I learnt so much from that friendship, the most important being never cover up for anyone no matter who they are.
If being thrown out of that door means I was fired then it means I have been fired twice in my life, both times because of women. Is it any wonder I turned out gay? I felt sad about the whole thing that had gone on in the salon with Julie but it had nothing to do with me. I missed Julie for a long time, but like any loss you get on with your own life, or at least try to.

I was married with a five year old child and now had no job. It wasn't a good position to be in. The town of Altrincham wasn't too far away from where we lived at the time so off I set in search of my next job. On walking up the high street I saw a beautiful salon with an advert in the window saying 'Full time stylist wanted'. Great, I thought.

You'll Never Make a Hairdresser

'Hi' I said to the receptionist.

'I was just passing and noticed the sign in the salon window advertising for a full time stylist'.

'If you can wait half an hour I'll get the manageress to see you'.

'Yes. Thanks, I can wait' I said.

Sitting having my coffee gave me the opportunity to have a good look around. I thought the salon was beautiful, but like so many other things in life appearances can be deceptive.

'Hello my name's Helen, I'm the manageress here, I believe you've come about the job?'

'Yes' I said.

'Then please come through into the office'.

After telling her what I was looking for and what I could do she asked

'Do you have pubic hair?'

'What?' I said.

'Do you have pubic hair?'

I didn't understand what she was going on about. I had just sat down with her to start my interview and she asks me if I have pubic hair. What the fuck was going on?

'Well yes' I said with a puzzled look on my face. Back then I don't think it was the thing to shave your pubic hair as it is today. Or if it was then I wasn't a follower of fashion. Not then anyway. She laughed aloud and said

'Just joking'.

I was ever more puzzled by then but after the interview I was told that I had the job and asked if I could start the following Tuesday. Arriving home I told my wife about the new job but didn't mention the pubic hair issue. Well it's not something you want to discuss with your wife, so I thought it was best just to forget it.

I loved the salon, it was buzzing. Everyone was so young and fashionable and it was where I wanted to be. I couldn't have wished for anywhere better to work. The only thing was the people there were always shagging. Whether it be staff, clients, you name it, if it had a pulse and looked half decent it was shagged. I'm not a prude, but I was married, and for all I loved the salon I wasn't fitting in well. There was no way I was going to shag anyone.

On one occasion when we were running out of coffee I went upstairs to where it was kept with all the other stock; tints, shampoos, perms. I ran up the stairs as quickly as I could and as I swung open the door to the stock room I nearly died of shock. There was my boss sitting on a box, with her legs wide open, knickers on the floor with a small perm bottle in her hand.

'Shut the fucking door' she shouted.

I shut the door that quickly I was surprised the door frame stayed up. I had never seen anything like it in all my life, nor might I add have I seen anything like it since. That was it I thought, I've had enough. I've put up with some shit in my life but this topped it all. I walked into the staff room, got my bag and went on the salon floor to get my things.

'Where are you going?' asked one of the staff.

'Home' I said.

'But the lady is still waiting in reception for her coffee' said the young girl.

'Well she'll be waiting a long fucking time' I said as I walk out of the salon.

I never even returned for the money they owed me. Throughout my life I have put up with being called every name under the sun, I have been hit, spat at punched and kicked, but never thank God have I, my brother or older sister ever been exposed to anything sexual.

I was lucky that I could cut men's hair as well as ladies and for those of you who think there is no difference, think again. I imagine most hairdressers can do a quick short back and sides on a man but when it comes to styling a mans hair it's nothing like cutting a lady's hair. With cutting men's hair there's usually a lot more precision cutting involved and you must be able to blend the hairline away into the nape of the neck, not just with clippers but using your scissors as well. Sure, there is a certain amount of precision cutting on women's hair too but by no means is it like cutting men's hair.

What I did learn about cutting men's hair is that you only get one chance to get in right. One wrong move and that's it, you have no choice but to try and talk your client into having a number one!
I've worked with some amazing stylists in my time but surprisingly half of them couldn't cut men's hair. I always found this a bit bizarre, but as with every trade we all have our own forte.

So it was another sign in another window, 'Barber required'. This time I got the job and loved it. There were seven guys in total, all stood in a row cutting hair all day long. Mark, myself and the owner were the only guys working in the salon who were 'straight'. Or were we?
The gay guys working there were not the stereotypical camp type, they looked as straight as any man that walked in for a hair cut. Most of the time we were all busy cutting but as soon as we were waiting around for men to come in that's when the fun would start. I never really got involved much with the gay men, not because I didn't like them but because it was at this time that I was starting to question my own sexuality, and this was something I wanted and needed to do alone.

We all had a good viewpoint from the salon to the main car park and this gave us all the opportunity to see who was parking up and who was about to call in the salon for a hair cut. If the client was handsome all hell let loose, the gay barbers would be screaming at each other like old women, all arguing over who would be cutting his hair. This often made me laugh because as soon as the guy walked into the salon they would all be nice and quiet and very professional. He had no idea that five of the guys had all been fighting for him.

The boss of the barbers was always nipping out for sex. He was shagging the landlady from the local pub as well as the pharmacy lady from a few shops down the lane. His wife used to be a model for a big modelling agency in Manchester. She was a beautiful woman, he really didn't deserve her. He would constantly tell us all how he was sex mad and that he must have sex every day. If anything I used to feel sorry for him (or should I say his wife).

The staff room wall was covered in pictures of naked gay men, the gay staff would put them there to wind up Mark, the salon owner and me. Mark used to go mad and each day he would stick his page three poster on the wall just to get his own back. Poor Mark, his pictures never lasted long and as soon as he walked out of the staff room one of the gay guys would tear it down. I wasn't used to any of this and if my wife had ever popped into the salon for a quiet chat there was no way I could have ever taken her and my child into the staff room; it was more like a sex shop in there.

Without letting on to any of them I too preferred the gay pictures on the wall, but I was married with one child and another on the way so what was I thinking? All I knew was that I preferred the company of the gay guys and loved hearing all the stories that they would all tell after their weekends out. It was so very different to my life.

The gay guys for all they were very nice didn't give a shit about being discreet. If they wanted to do something they did it whether you were there or not. The staff room was tiny and most of the time we all had to have lunch sat around a small table. I had only been there a few days when one of the gay guys said

'Right, stay if you want but I'm having a wank'.

I couldn't believe what I was hearing. Martin jumped up, shouting.

'You dirty bastard! Why do you always do that in work? For fuck's sake, I'm going for the boss'

But this didn't stop him. By the time I stood up and started trying to get from behind the table he was already going for it, being egged on by the other gay guys that were still in the staff room.

You'll Never Make a Hairdresser

I didn't know what the hell to do. I know I should have run out of the staff room as quick as Mark had done but half of me had wanted to stay. As I left the staff room I knew I was doing the right thing. The boss stormed into the staff room and minutes later and after lots of shouting the gay guy finally stopped what he was doing. This behaviour continued however and in the end most of us learnt to just laugh it off. Mark on the other hand never found it funny, he always ran straight out of the staff room. I was always the last guy to leave the staff room. I wonder why?

Saturday was always a funny day. There was a young girl aged about 18 or 19 who fancied the boss and as you can imagine he well took advantage of her. She used to call into the salon all the time and in the end, guess what?
Yes, he was shagging her! She would work all day on a Saturday for nothing, well not quite nothing. Yes you've guessed it, need I say more? I thought it was so sad the way she was used but at the end of the day she was the one allowing it.

One of the gay guys had just come home from Spain and when he came back to work all he talked about was how he had fallen in love with a Spanish man he'd met. We all knew nothing would ever come of it but he seemed happy. He would constantly tell us all about his new man and sometimes in far too much detail. Mark was always so funny shouting at him, but it made no difference, he would just go on and on.

One day he came in to work and asked me if I would take a picture of him so he could send it to Spain to his new boyfriend.

'Yes' I said.

'Well, it's not really of me' he said, 'but of my penis'.

'What? Your penis!'

'Yes please, I don't want the other gay guys looking at me and I know Mark would never take it for me'.

'But why don't you take it yourself?' I asked.

'Because I want to dress it up a bit for him. Oh please Russ, it will only take a minute'.

'OK' I said.

With that he produced from his bag a can of shaving foam and a pair of dark glasses.

'What are you doing?' I asked.

'Oh it's just a joke between me and him,' he said.

Without saying any more he pulled down his pants and began slapping his penis very gently, saying

'Come on babe, we can't let your daddy see you like this now can we?'

'Look, I should go' I said, embarrassed.

'No, no we're nearly ready' he said as he started spraying the shaving foam all over his testicles. Once he'd done this he then placed the dark sun glasses on the top of his penis. I could not believe what was happening. What am I doing, I thought? Me a married man, stood in the staff room with a gay guy with his pants down, his balls smothered in shaving cream and a pair of dark sunglasses resting on top of his cock.

'Come on' he shouted.

'Oh yeah sorry' I found myself just standing there in a trance.

'Make sure you take a few just in case I don't like them'

The camera was one of the old instant types where the picture came out of the bottom, so by the time I had taken two or three pictures the shaving cream had started to drip all over the place. The pictures looked so funny when they all came out. The mad thing was he wouldn't let any of the other gay guys take his picture but he didn't mind them seeing them once they had been taken.

You'll Never Make a Hairdresser

When we'd all finished work that day he put one of his cock pictures in Mark's bag before he left to go home. We all had a good laugh with the exception of poor Mark who never did find it funny.

By now I was starting I think about opening my own salon. I had been saving hard and thought now was as good a time to do it than any. When I told everyone I was leaving they all felt sad, but I knew I was ready and had made my mind up. After giving my notice in my leaving date was fixed. Within days I found out that Mark was also leaving and he too had decided to open his own salon not too far away from where we were all already working. This didn't go down at all well with the salon owner and by the end of the day Mark had been paid off and told not to return back to work. This happens a lot in salons; if you are moving far away you would be asked to stay and work right up until your leaving date, but If the salon owner finds out that your new job or even your own salon isn't too far away then you are told to leave, usually as soon as you give your notice in.

The reason for this is to prevent you from telling your clients about your new job/ salon and where you will be working. I have worked with many a stylist who would never tell their employers they were leaving until their very last day. This way the stylists would have time to tell their clients where and when they would be going. I have also seen stylists log into the salon computer and download their client lists and telephone numbers. Usually they have no idea they are breaking data protection law and could also be prosecuted for stealing.

This nearly always happens. Staff come to work for you, they build up their clientele and think they can then open their own salon. I've seen it work out well on occasions, but more often than not it fails. What these hairdressers forget is when the customer first came into the salon, she came there because she may have been recommended, or she liked the look of the salon, and not because their name was above the door.

It was strange how it worked out but both Mark and I opened our own salons on the very same day. He opened his barbers not too far from where I lived and I opened my salon not too away far from his home. It wasn't planned, it was just the way it worked out. We both visited each other when ever we could. Most of the time I would go and cut his hair for him because he worked alone and there was no one else there to cut his hair. This had gone on for over a year when one day Mark call at my house on his way home from work and told me he hadn't been well. He was having the next day off work so he could go and have a check up at the local hospital.

Being in the same business I knew he would lose a lot of money and maybe clients if he was to just close his salon for the day. Because my salon had a team of staff I was able to arrange for my column to be covered so that I could take the following day off in order to help Mark out by opening his salon for him. So the next day I found myself working in Mark's barbers shop; it wasn't for the money and I made sure he had it all in his till at the end of the day. I did it for him because I knew if I was the one needing help he'd be there for me in any way he could.

I was so glad I did. Mark and his Mother came to see me a few days later, and the news was not good. Mark had cancer. I was devastated; he was only 23 and had his whole life to look forward to. We talked about his illness and his business and Mark said he wanted to carry on working for as long as he could. The first thing we did was to get him some staff. My salon was over twenty miles away from his barbers, on a good run this could take me an hour to get over to him. He would often call me up telling he had to go home as he was feeling unwell. I'd get hold of his staff and try and sort out cover for his barber's salon. It was a hard time for all of us, and if the staff couldn't cover then I used to find cover for my own salon just to keep Mark's open.

The news came that Mark had only a few months to live, and despite all the hard work from everyone involved Marks barber's business had to be closed. It was so very, very sad. Mark went to live with his parents in Cornwall, and his home was put up for sale. I went around to his house the day before he was due to leave; all his things had been packed up and there were names on most of his boxes.

'What have you done this for?' I asked.

'Because I want my mother to give each box of things away to the right person. She'll only get it wrong if their names are not on them' he said smiling.

'This is for you' he said, as he handed me a C D of Jonathan Butler.

We smiled. This was the C D that was always played in the salon that we had first met in. We would both moan because it was constantly played. As he handed it to me he said

'I want to thank you for all the things that you have done for me and I want you to know you have and always will be the only gay man that I have loved'

'But I'm not gay' I said.

'You might be able to fool others Russ but you can't fool me. You have a life Russell; make sure you live it as you want to live it, not as others wish you to'.

As I was leaving we both knew we would never see each other again. I will always remember him standing in his door way smiling holding his front door open for me saying

'Go on, piss off you fucking Queer'.

Mark died four months later. He was 24.

Allyson

Who was she? Where is she? And Why? I ask these questions to myself over and over again every single day of my life.

Who was she? The answer is that she was the most beautiful person I had ever met. She's the person who showed me so much love, she was so caring and always did whatever she could for others. If I was ever faced with any kind of trouble she would take me by the hand and walk one step ahead of me, taking on my behalf whatever was coming my way. She was the only woman I would ever send a mother's day card to, and to me she was my sister, mother and best friend all rolled into one. Others knew her as Allyson, Russell's sister.

Where is she? Allyson died on the 9th of March 1997, she was thirty six years old. As well as being the saddest day of my life to date it was the day my life would change forever.

Why did she die? Only God knows.

At this moment in time I don't want to go into too much detail about Allyson simply because I believe her life deserves a book dedicated to her alone. A book that I plan to write as soon as this one is finished. It will tell of the life she had, the pain she went through and all the people who should have been there for her but never were.

At the time Allyson was diagnosed with her illness I was working in Hale, Cheshire. I was driving back and forth from my house in North Wales which was an exhausting journey of 134 miles a day, which doesn't sound that bad if you say it quickly! I realise this was my own choice but I felt at that time I wanted to live in a nicer place with my own family, a place where my own children would feel healthier, safer and I hoped, a lot happier. Working in a town like Hale I was able to make good money from hairdressing. Although I wasn't working in the centre of Manchester, Hale had a lot of very wealthy people who were prepared to pay a good price to have their hair cut and styled.

The Christmas of 1996 was as busy as every other Christmas in any

You'll Never Make a Hairdresser

hairdressing salon and I couldn't wait to finish so I could head off home and spend a few days off with my own family. Closing time finally came, and once the salon had closed it was time for all the staff to swap their Christmas gifts and wish each other a happy time. With that done I had just enough time to nip in to see Allyson and her family before finally heading off home myself. By now Allyson was living in Manchester with her partner and her four young children and she was pregnant with her fifth child.

Tommy (my older brother) Allyson and me were so close; never a day passed by without one of us popping around to see the other. We were our own small, close knit family and our lives were committed to looking out for each other. After seeing Allyson and her family I jumped back in the car and onto the motorway back home to North Wales. I will always remember us all having a wonderful Christmas that year. Everyone had a great time and lots of fun, especially the children. The house where I lived in North Wales had quite a bit of ground to it and within the grounds was a small forest of Christmas trees which provided the backdrop to such a wonderful time. I remember myself and my daughter going out in the snow looking for the best tree to bring home, at the same time reinforcing in my mind exactly why I was spending so much time driving up and down that bloody motor way. I knew it was all worth it.

New Year's Eve was another busy time for the salon, but after just having some time at home I was ready for the hard work to begin again. After having dinner the evening before New Years Eve I decided to pack my car with the things that I needed to take back to the salon with me when I started to experience a really bad pain in my head. By the time I had packed the car and made my way to the front door of the house my headache was so intense it felt like my head was going to explode. This had happened so fast and just before I was able to step inside the house I vomited violently all over the front step. I had never known a pain like this nor one to attack me so suddenly.

Thinking I was having a bad migraine I said I would go and have a lie down to see if the pain would clear, so off I went to my room. At about 11.30 that night I woke up in my daughter's bedroom screaming in pain. Luckily my doctor only lived a stone's throw away and he came around right away. He gave me an injection to stop the pain which also helped me drift back to sleep again. Settling down I knew that my wife would call the salon early the next morning to explain to them why I wasn't going to be in work.

Amazingly when I woke up the next morning I felt fine. I couldn't believe I felt so well given the excruciating pain that I'd had the previous night. Never in all my life had I felt such pain. I have had epilepsy for ten years now and never in all this time have I felt that level of pain, but waking up so well that morning made me feel as if the night before had never happened.

By 7.30 I was on the motorway heading back to the salon in Cheshire. I was just putting all the salon lights on when the phone rang. The lady on the other end of the phone advised that she was calling from the local hospital. She told me that Allyson was unwell and had been admitted the night before. I waited until the staff got into work and explained that I had to go to my sister. I knew I had a full column that day and all the ladies would be expecting their hair done by me but there was nothing I could do. I had to go to Allyson.

When I walked into her room at the hospital she was just sat in bed looking healthy and well. 'What's gone on?' I asked. Allyson started to explain what had happened to her the night before. As she was talking she was also describing exactly what had happened to me at home in North Wales; it was as if she had been there with me and was describing what I had gone through. She had called an ambulance for herself because she was worried about the child she was carrying. I didn't tell her that I too had been unwell in the night because I didn't want to worry her while she was in the hospital.

I had heard of people feeling unwell at the same time before but thought that kind of coincidence only happened to twins. How could this have happened to me and Allyson? After I left her in the hospital I couldn't stop thinking about how we had both had the same pain in our heads at the same time. For me the pain had gone but for Allyson the pain was only just beginning.

After spending a few days in hospital undergoing tests Allyson was allowed home. The doctors said they were putting the headache down to the fact that she had high blood pressure and that she was carrying a child. I called to see her that night after work and she looked really well. Now that the worry had gone I joked to her that she had only called the ambulance so she could have a rest at the hospital! Three days later Allyson was back in hospital. The pains in her head had returned and this time she had suffered an epileptic fit which was something she had never had before. More tests were carried out and by the end of the day Allyson was diagnosed with brain cancer. She was given six to eight weeks to live. Looking back now I realise that we (Allyson, Tommy and myself) were in total shock; we just sat there for hours holding each other without saying a word. She never cried or screamed, she just kept hold of us. Now and then she would give us a tighter hug and a kiss followed by one of her amazing smiles.

Finally Allyson said

'Look you two. Listen to me'

Tommy and I just sat there staring at her as she spoke.

'I believe that the doctors must have it all wrong. There is no way that God would allow me to conceive this child and not give birth to it. He wouldn't take me away from my other four children now would he? And if he does then he must have one hell of a vacancy for me! I want us all to carry on as normal'

I couldn't stop crying. Inside I was screaming but I didn't let her see that.

'Come on now Russell, stop crying. You'll only set me off. There's no way I'll ever leave you two'

The next few weeks were a living hell. I had my family who were in North Wales, my salon in Cheshire and my dying sister who was living in Manchester. I don't know how I did it, but for weeks I crammed all three into one day, every day. Without Allyson knowing, me and my brother were having meetings with the doctors to see if anything could be done. During one of the discussions it was agreed that the unborn child would have to be born. Allyson was never going to last until the date the child was due. How do you ask your sister to let go of her unborn child?

The date was agreed and on the 14th of February Allyson's beautiful baby girl was born by caesarean section. Allyson was far too weak to go and see the baby who was fighting for its own life in intensive care. When she gained consciousness she couldn't believe she had had another baby girl. Tommy and myself went to see her daughter and took pictures of her so that we were able to show her, and with the exception of a very few brief visits this was the only way she could see her baby.

Allyson died just four weeks after she had given life to her beautiful daughter. It was Mother's day, the 9th of March 1997. Again Tommy and I were with her, we had never left her side for three days. After she died we stayed with her as long as we could, we just couldn't bear to say good bye. How could we? We couldn't believe that our young beautiful sister was lying there dead and at the same time her own baby was still fighting for its own life just a few feet away in intensive care. As I kissed my sister good bye I knew my own life would never be the same again. How could it? I could never describe to anyone in just a few sentences how I ever got through the weeks and months that followed, so I won't even try. The family rows, the children, the court case and of course the funeral. I will leave all of these things for the book I will write for my sister one day.

 I would like to share with you the poem I wrote for my sister a few days after she had died.

You'll Never Make a Hairdresser

We should have known in the beginning, that your life would have had a twist.

It started off with two unknown people, who only thought they'd kissed.

The shock and the horror seemed too much to bear. Two more children down the line, there must have been love there.

In the beginning it was rocky, but the years did go by.

We would meet chat about them, sometimes laugh, sometimes cry.

March 1997 was the hardest time of all, your mind was working overtime as your heart beat began to fall.

I shall never forget the moment that your eyes locked onto mine, we didn't speak, we couldn't hear, I knew you were reading my mind.

The funeral came and went, the lingers on were standing by.

There was nothing I could give as your memories were all mine.

We made a pact I will defend until the very end.

I left when you were sleeping, I'll see you when you awake.

We have too much love inside of us for anyone to break.

They gave me life, you gave me hope.

I know how to love because you loved me.

I know how to care because you've shown me.

I feel pain because you left me.

I have two eyes so you can see.

I have two ears so you can hear.

You have and always will be in my heart.

What ever I do in my life is your doing.

My life, your life, is our life.

Time to move on

Six months had passed since Allyson's death. Although my own life was carrying on, it was far from normal. I remember getting off the train one day in Chester station and realising that I had left my car in the salon car park back in Hale, Cheshire. Why had I done this? All the years I had been travelling between home and work I had never once got the train. I had no idea why I had got on that train that night, all I knew was that I had no option but to get back on it and head back to my car in Cheshire. I lived that far away from the train station in North Wales I would have needed my car in any case. The whole time I was travelling to Chester it had never crossed my mind that I had walked past my car. After finally picking the car up I found myself driving back home in the dark to North Wales and knew I was going to be so late getting home.

I don't know what was going through my mind, but the next minute I was in floods of tears. If anyone had asked me what was wrong I couldn't have told them because I didn't know. Was it the fact that I'd forgotten my car or the fact that I was just tired from work? Maybe I'll never know. I was crying that much it got to the point that I found it hard to see and even breathe. I pulled over in the next lay by. Getting out of the car was like stepping into a shower, the rain was coming down so hard but I didn't care, I had to get out and get some fresh air. Walking away from my car, I started to scream. I found myself screaming at the top of my voice, Why? Why? Why?

I realised I was asking God why had he taken my sister away from me? I looked at my watch; it was twelve thirty and I wasn't even half way home. When I finally got home I sat down and told my wife what had gone on at the train station and how I'd been upset on the way home. We knew then that I needed some time off, but it was now October and over the next few weeks the salon would be getting ready again for Christmas.

Within hours I found myself back on the motorway getting ready to start my day all over again. The staff were good but there was only so much I wanted to tell them. Over the following few weeks my life went by in one big blur. Friday night came and as always at eight O' Clock I told my staff I was off home and that I would see them in the morning.

You'll Never Make a Hairdresser

If anything I seem to remember that week being one of my good weeks. Once home and after tea my wife and I sorted the girls out with their bits and bobs then we all sat down as normal to watch some T.V. I remember my wife going up to bed first and within an hour or so I was in bed too. The next thing I remember was my wife standing over me asking if I was OK. As I looked around the room I could see two ambulance men, they were talking to me but I felt as if they were whispering and I couldn't really hear them. When I tried talking back to them I could hear myself talking a load of rubbish and the more I tried to speak the more silly I sounded. What was happening to me? I was getting so scared I began to panic. I tried to get up from my bed but the ambulance men held me back down asking me not to move.

'We believe you've had an epileptic fit in your sleep, just lie down as still as you can while we sort you out' said one of the ambulance men.

I just lay there in total shock, my head was banging and my body felt like it had been hit by a bus. Then there was the smell. It looked like my whole inside was lying there with me, I couldn't believe what was happening, and all the time I was thinking no I can't have had a fit, not me.

The next thing I remember was waking up in the ambulance and the ambulance man saying

'You're OK now mate, don't worry you're on your way to hospital. We'll sort you out when we get there. You just lie still'

As I lay there in the ambulance the first thing that came into my head was my sister Allyson. Did I have the same as her? Was I going to die of cancer too? What about my children? What about her children? What about my brother and my wife? What about my life?

I could feel the tears running down my face but because I was strapped to the bed I couldn't move, I couldn't even wipe my own tears away.

'It's OK mate' said the ambulance man as he wiped away my tears. 'Don't you worry, we'll have you ship shape in no time'.

My wife, father and brother came to visit me the next day. No one could understand why this had happened but every test was being carried out on me to make sure there was no cancer. I stayed in the local hospital for two weeks but because I'd been having more fits I was sent by ambulance to a specialist hospital in Liverpool. The whole time I felt like I was living in a dream that I couldn't wake myself up from. The tests were back, and my wife, brother and father all waited for the doctors to come and speak to us. It seemed like the longest wait we'd ever had.

'First things first' said the doctor as he sat down. 'you're not going to die, not yet anyway and not because of this illness. What you have is epilepsy'.

I still didn't understand. Why now? Why me? I sat there as my family asked the doctor all sorts of questions. I think I'd switched off when I heard the word epilepsy, I just wanted to get up and run as far away from everyone as possible. Not that I would have got very far, because at the time I had about twenty or thirty wires glued onto my scalp that were attached to a small device strapped around my waist. It was worse than living in a dream. It was a nightmare and I was living it.

'It will be a complete life change for a while, but as soon as we sort his tablets out his fits will stabilise' said the doctor.

I just sat there and cried. Everyone in the room was saying how good the news was. Yes, looking back it was good news, it could have been a lot worse, but to me it felt like the end of my life. I was thirty, I now had no job, no car, no driving licence and was too scared to walk up the stairs alone in case I had an other fit. Yeah, what a great life!

I soon realised I wasn't scared of the fits, although they were bad it was the falls that always did more damage than anything. In the months that followed I suffered a broken nose, broken ribs and head cuts, many of which I couldn't remember. How much worse could it get? I ended up in hospital the first time for seven weeks.

At this time I also felt so sorry for all the staff who were left in the salon and I still think about them to this day. The main stylist was offered to buy the salon but she couldn't afford it and within eight weeks the salon had closed. I never returned to that salon after telling the staff 'I'll see you in the morning'; how wrong I was. The main stylist had agreed to run the salon until I was able to return but I think the thought of me being off for so long must have frightened her. After running the salon for eight years most of my staff had now left, so sadly we had no choice but to close the salon down. Shame.

When I was finally allowed home, I found it difficult just being in the house doing nothing. The beautiful house in the country that I longed for all those years before had in the end become the worst place on earth for me. I felt so isolated, money was now very tight, the school run alone was taking forty minutes and my wife was now the only driver in the house. Some days she would have to stay out all day because we couldn't afford the petrol for her to keep coming home. This was also difficult for her because she was having to find something to do all day and usually with no money.

I on the other hand would be sat at home all day feeling sorry for myself, slowly getting more and more depressed. I couldn't even pluck up the courage to walk a short distance for the paper or a bottle of milk because of the fear of having a fit and lying there in the road. The fits were still happening maybe once or twice a day, and the worst thing was not knowing when they were going to happen. The doctors were still coming out to see me, and by now we had a family social worker who would try and help with things. She once asked me 'Is there anything I can get you that would make you and your family's life better?' I replied 'Just give me my health, I'll get them the rest' but of course for all the things she could get us, health was the one thing she couldn't get.

It was suggested that I might benefit from the help of a bereavement counsellor, someone to talk to about the loss of my sister. I agreed and Mr Paul Jones walked into my life.

At first Mr Jones would come to visit me at the house, we would talk about everything and nothing; I found it very hard to just talk to someone that I had only just met. Sometimes my wife would be asked to sit in on our chats but mostly I was alone with him. I felt that my life and mind were so messed up at this time I couldn't have told you what day it was, never mind the year. I found myself taking so much medication that sometimes I was asleep for days at a time. When I was awake I was no good to anyone, I walked around the house like a zombie, but the more I told the doctors I wasn't feeling well the more medication I was prescribed.

With the fits, depression and sleeping tablets I was now taking 16 tablets a day. I told the doctors that I wasn't used to taking tablets and asked about the harm they might do to me. Keep taking them was all I got told.

It was November when my wife woke up in the night and found that I wasn't in bed beside her. Looking around the house I was nowhere to be found. On noticing the patio doors open she grabbed her coat and went outside. There I lay naked and fast asleep curled up in the freezing cold. When she woke me up I had no knowledge of how I had got there. Although she was shocked I was totally freaked out. We got back into bed and tried to forget all about it. About three nights later the same thing happened again, only this time when my wife got up from bed she wasn't able to find me anywhere.

She called the police and luckily for me when the police were making their way to our house they spotted me walking along the dark country lanes, again naked and about three miles way from my home. Why was this happening to me and where was I heading?

The police told my wife there was no way they could get me into the police van because I hadn't ever been aware they were with me.
In the end they had to drive the van in front of me and open the doors. According to their report I carried on walking and went straight into the back of the van. When they opened the van back at the police station I was still walking, still unaware of where I was. The police said they could not take me back home to my family without seeing a doctor first. When the doctor arrived I was given an injection and taken to our local hospital.

When I eventually woke up I was told yet again what had been going on. Shocked was an understatement; how could someone do all those things and not even be aware of it? What was happening to me? The doctors said they could only put it down to my medication and that it was best for me to stay in the hospital until they had managed to sort it out.

You'll Never Make a Hairdresser

My wife and brother were constantly at the hospital and my father would visit whenever he could. I was sat alone one day when a nurse came over to me chatting. She asked,

'I know you talk about your sister a lot Russell, would it not help if you talked about your mother as well?'

'But why?' I replied

'Well when we lose someone that we love, it helps to talk about them' she said.

'But my mother's not dead' I replied.

'Oh, then where is she, why has she never been to see you after all this time? She must know how poorly you have been.' she asked.

'Please nurse, don't ask' I replied.

How could I say I had two mothers and that neither gave a shit about anyone but themselves.

My medication was taking its time to kick in. Some medication was taken away and more was given. I was still questioning all the medication I was taking, but I was assured that I was doing the right thing by taking it. The doctors know best, yeah?

My family (Dad, Tommy and my wife) were told that I had started sleepwalking because my mind couldn't rest (this was a joke).They said because of the shock of losing my sister, my job and then with the added shock of starting with the epilepsy it had all became too much for me and my body was fighting back. I found myself feeling more and more low, the thought of walking around all day scared me in case I was to have an other fit and now I found myself scared of going to sleep in case I ended up dead in a ditch somewhere. All I wanted to do was go home with my wife and children, get well, get a job and be as happy as anyone could be, was that asking too much?

The hospital had decided they were going to have to give me my own room because I was disturbing the other patients on the ward by getting up in the night. Mr Jones continued to see me all the time I was in hospital; we would sit and chat, but to me the only thing I felt after he'd gone was even more sadness. Maybe he was right, all he wanted to talk about was my past, something I strongly wanted to forget, but what was happening then was far more important to me than my past.

After two weeks in the local hospital I had walked in my sleep three or four times. One day I went for a lie down in the afternoon and the next thing I remembered was being woken up by a nurse. I could hear the sound of laughter as I sat up, the nurse didn't look familiar to me and why should she; I was on a different ward three floors up, again naked. Then I heard another patient say

'I'll have whatever he's had nurse'

As I looked around I noticed visitors sitting by their loved ones; it was visiting time. They had all seen me walk into the room naked and climb into some else's bed. I had got out of my own bed, walked out of my ward, got into a lift and walked on to an other ward and climbed into this guy's bed. How is this possible? I ask you; why had no one seen me? I couldn't believe what was happening. I told my wife and the doctors that I didn't want to stay in the hospital any more. I wanted to go home. I was asked to attend a meeting with the doctors the following day and then they would let me go home.

'No I've had enough, I want to go home now' I said

'I promise you, let me sort out your medication and by the morning you'll be on your way home' The doctor replied.

The next day my wife came to meet me and we both went down to see the doctor as planed. As I walked into the room I was shocked to see so many people there. Mr Jones was there, my social worker and other doctors who I hadn't seen before. After my doctor had asked us to sit down he started to introduce the other people in the room. Just then there was a knock at the door and in walked my father and brother. I was so shocked to see them, what were they doing here? As I got up and walked towards them I said

You'll Never Make a Hairdresser

'Hi, what are you doing here? I'm just sorting out my medication with the doctors and then I'm off home, you can wait here or I'll meet you at my house, I shouldn't be that long now'

'Please Russell, sit down' said Mr Jones, 'I've asked your father and brother to come today'

'But why?' I asked, still standing in the middle of the room with everyone looking at me.

'Please Russell, just sit down' Mr Jones replied.

As I walked back to my seat I started to feel sick. I was sure that the doctors had found something else wrong with me, I could feel everyone staring at me. My father and brother had never even spoken, they didn't even answer me when they came into the room and they both just sat there with their heads looking down.

I couldn't help it, as I looked over at my wife I asked

'What is it, what's wrong with me?'

'We have a slight problem Russell' replied one of the doctors that I'd never seen before. 'We don't believe that at this time it would be in your best interest to go back home'

'Well I'm going' I shouted as I jumped out of my seat 'Anyway who are you to say that, you're not even my doctor' Turning to Mr Jones and my own doctor I said

'Well go on you tell him, tell him he's wrong'

Dad walked towards me and put his arms around me, he asked me to sit back down and listen to what the people in the room had to say.

Walking to my seat I said ' I don't give a fuck what they say, I'm fucking going home'

One of the ladies in the room said she was from the welfare, she went on to explain that because there were children at my place it wouldn't be safe for me or them if I returned home at this time.

Looking back I should have stayed more calm but I didn't, I went off my head. 'They are my children' I said, 'and I want to go home to them!'

They were having none of it. They felt because of the fits I was still experiencing and the sleep walking there was no way that my wife could look after me and the children. The doctors had decided they were not allowing me to go home.

Everyone in the room was talking across each other. I couldn't understand what was going on or what was being said. I just wanted to be allowed to go home, but there was no way out. The doctors explained that because of the sleep walking I wouldn't be allowed to stay in the local hospital because I was putting myself and others in danger. He went on to say the only place I could go was to the local psychiatric hospital where I would be appointed someone to sit with me at all times, even when I was sleeping.

I just sat there numb. My father and brother started shouting at everyone. I remember looking around the room through tears that were running down my face. The way everyone was looking at me I knew they all thought I was stark raving mad, but they didn't know me, none of them did; I had a life before I had met any of them, a good life, and who were they to say I couldn't go home? I knew if I was to start shouting like my poor brother I would be falling right into their hands. I just sat there absolutely shitting myself.

By the end of the meeting it was decided I would be allowed to go and stay with my father back in Manchester, but I couldn't go to my own home without the doctors say so. I agreed to still come and see Mr Jones every week and to keep all my appointments at the hospital regarding my epilepsy. I would have agreed to anything, all I wanted was to get out of that place. I didn't care what the conditions were, I just wanted out.

Some nights without the hospital knowing I would go and stay with my brother and his family. I was grateful to Dad and my brother for all they had done for me, but I still wanted to go home. I was thirty and being passed from pillar to post. I wanted something of my own again, I wanted my life back.

Everything I had ever worked for had gone, even my own family. My father and brother had tried to hide the fact that I was still sleep walking, and for that I will always be very grateful, but the fact was it was still happening. Dad said he got up one morning at five to go to work and I had gone. The clothes I was wearing the day before were on the floor, so he knew I had gone out with nothing on. He had no choice but to call the police.

The police told him they already had a young man in custody that fitted my description. I didn't know this at the time but have since been told that sometimes people who walk in their sleep tend to walk in straight lines. This would explain how I was spotted walking around and around a roundabout in the heart of Manchester. When my brother and father picked me up from the police station I felt both sad and mad at the same time. I knew it wasn't fair for them to have to put up with all this, and so it was decided we should call Mr Jones who in turn got in touch with the hospital back in North Wales.

The next day I was driven back to the hospital for another meeting with my doctors. Once there they told me if I didn't agree to go into the psychiatric hospital they would have the doctors section me under the mental heath act. They went on to say they didn't for one minute believe I was mad, but because of the sleep walking there was nowhere else for me to go; 'It's for your own protection', they said.

I was told I could have my own room and wouldn't have to mix with anyone in there. 'If you come voluntarily Russell I will allow you to have as many visitors as you like. If I have to section you, I will see to it you have none. It's up to you.' This meant that come rain or shine I wouldn't get out of there within twenty eight days.

As I got up and walked over to the window I could hear my brother and father crying. Looking out of the window I could see my daughter being pushed on one of the swings in the hospital grounds. What choice did I have? I had nowhere else to go. I was scared of being alone, I was scared of going to sleep and scared of going out alone in case I had another fit. As I turned around I could see my family crying when I said

'OK I'll go, but when?'

'Now' said the doctor.

My brother was screaming, 'No, no, I'll have him at my house, please don't take him'

With tears running down my face I said my goodbyes to my family and walked out of the room with the doctors. It was two days before New Years Eve 1997.

I had no idea what to expect, but when I got to the psychiatric hospital, apart from every door being locked behind me I thought it looked like a hotel, two star I might add! I was shown to my room and I must say it was very, very nice. Apart from the bars on the windows and the odd scream coming from somewhere in the building I would never have believed I was in a psychiatric hospital. Mr Jones still came to see me and my family were always there. Thank God they were because I never once, in all the time I was there, went for anything to eat. I didn't want to mix with the others in there. I could hear them and that was enough.

The doctors soon noticed I wasn't going to the canteen for my food and said 'We will not bring the food to you, you have to go and get it yourself.'
I think they thought I would go in the end but in all the weeks I stayed in there, I never ever went in. In fact I never had any of their food, not even once. I'm sure it was very nice, but it was the thought of having to mix with the others that put me off. My poor brother brought in everything I needed.

The fits were slowly starting to be controlled, but my sleep walking still remained a concern. Maybe it was happening once or twice a week now, but there was no way I was going to be discharged until it had stopped completely. My chats with Mr Jones were getting more and more intense; I'd gone though my childhood and found that part very upsetting, and then he started to work through my thoughts about my sister Allyson which was again very upsetting. I had to be so truthful with him; I told him things I would only ever have told my sister and this also included the fact that I was gay. We would chat about this for hours and he said I would not start to get or feel better by keeping all this to myself, but there was no way I was going to tell my wife and family I was gay, how could I?

You'll Never Make a Hairdresser

As the weeks passed I started to accept that the fits were here to stay and if I could keep them under control by taking the medication then there was a way I could try and get my life back. I missed my life, I had worked so hard for what I had and now it had all gone. I knew I would have to start all over again. It was the sleep walking I had to get rid of. Slowly this occurred less frequently, so much so that in one of my weekly meetings with the doctors I asked if or when I could go home. The answer was always the same; 'Next week Russell', they would say.

I felt that although they were the doctors, and good at their jobs, they still didn't know me or what type of person I was. I didn't want to be there. I wasn't like other people in there, I knew some people in there were mad and needed help with their minds but all I wanted from the doctors was some help to stop my sleep walking. I felt sorry for some of the people in the psychiatric hospital, there were some nice people and very sad people who for whatever reason had something wrong with their minds. It didn't make them any less a person for having a mental illness, but even so I didn't want to go and have dinner at the same table as them.

Again I wanted to go home and had asked that much that another meeting was called my family were all invited to attend. It was agreed by all the doctors that I was ready to go home, but it would still be too much work for my wife if I was to return back to her house at that particular time.

Manchester was too far away for me to still attend my meeting with Mr Jones, so for me to go and stay with my family there was out of the question.

'It looks like you'll have to stay here a little while longer' said the doctors.

I screamed 'No, I have done all what was asked of me, why can't you let me go?'

'There is still nowhere for you to go Russell, no one is able to look after you at this time, we have no choice but to keep you here for a few more weeks and then we'll meet again' said the doctors.

I ran over to my father.

'Dad you tell them, I can come and live with you, please Dad tell them.'

But with tears in his eyes he began shaking his head from side to side. Running over to my wife I yelled

'You tell them I'm OK and I can come home with you, I'll help you with the kids you'll be able to cope, please tell them, go on please'

The more I pleaded the louder I got until in the end I must have looked just like all the other people in there. I felt such a fool, I wanted to scream but it would have done me no good, if anything it would have done me more harm. Sad, I dried my eyes looked at my family and said

'It's OK, I understand, thanks anyway'

I couldn't wait until I got out of that room. I'd made myself look mad, just like many of the people in that room thought I was; the way I was begging them to let me go home. I was so desperate to show them that I was feeling better, but I'd blown it, if anything I felt I had just confirmed what they all felt, that I was going mad. Maybe I was, but they couldn't see that they were actually making me feel the way I did. I didn't know what I was going to do. I had to stop this sleep walking before I was going to get out of there, there was no way they were going to let me go until it stopped. I was still taking all the medication that was being given to me and the only thing I could see slowing down was the fits.

Weeks had passed by as I lay on my bed thinking what I could do to stop the sleep walking once and for all. Then I figured out that before the doctors had given me all the medication I had been OK, apart from the fitting. Without telling anyone I stopped taking my tablets. The only medication I took was for my fits, everything else went down my sink. I had tried flushing them down the toilet but they wouldn't go down, so within days my small hand sink was blocked. I remember shitting myself in case they found out what I'd been doing so the time came to find a new place for my tablets to go.

You'll Never Make a Hairdresser

Because I was still fitting I was constantly being observed in the day and because of the sleep walking I was being supervised at night. My brother had just bought me a new jacket for Christmas and it hung up in my wardrobe ready for me to wear when I eventually got out so I started to use the jacket to hide my tablets in. Within a few days I was feeling so much better, I knew I was doing the right thing. The next meeting I had with the doctors I told them how much better I was feeling and again knew I felt I was ready to go home.

'You keep this up Russell' said the doctors yet again 'and you'll be going home very soon.'

By now I was starting to believe it, I could see home in sight. All the time my family still came to see me. It had been a fortnight since I had walked in my sleep, never had I gone that long since I was in their hospital; I was now convinced the cause had been all the medication that they had been giving me. The next meeting with the doctors went very well and they were all very impressed with me. When I got to my room my brother and my wife were there waiting to visit me. They were so happy for me, telling me how great I was doing and how all the doctors said I would be OK in the end.

'I know that you both believe in what the doctors say but please hear me out' I said.

I went on to tell them that I'd not been taking my tablets for the past few weeks and how I was finding it hard to get rid of them. They both just sat there quiet, listening to what I was saying.

'I know I'm right, I haven't felt this well in a long time, even the doctors are saying I'll be home soon.'

'But you've been given this medication for a reason Russell, and if you don't take it then the sleep walking might come back again' said my wife.

'Tommy, come on tell her, I'm doing the right thing yeah, you know I am don't you?'

'I need you to help me get rid of the tablets, I have so many of them and I have nowhere else to put them'

'No' said my brother 'we can't do that, you must get rid of them yourself'

My wife stood up and walking to the wardrobe said. 'I'll get rid of them for you but please don't tell anyone what I've done, will you?'

'No' I said thanking her.

I felt so much better when they had left and I was glad I had told them about the medication. I knew I could trust them. I was just about to lie on my bed when my bedroom door flew open. I jumped in shock thinking one of the mad inmates had some how got into my room but I was mistaken. There standing in my door way were three huge men and behind them a doctor.

'Turn around and face the fucking wall!!!!!!' one of them shouted.

I wished at this point that one of the inmates had entered my room instead of those three.
I was that shocked I just stood there staring at them all when he shouted again.

'I said fucking turn around now!!!!!!'

'Why?' I shouted back.

Wrong thing to say I thought, as all three men ran at me. It was like being attacked by three gorillas, they even sounded like them the way they roared as they were running towards me. I didn't have time to change my mind and do as they had asked, I was smashed against the wall, turned upside down and punched and kicked at the same time.
Within seconds my hands were behind my back and tied to my feet. Of course I was constantly screaming for them to get off me but I believe under all their roaring no one could even hear me.

You'd have thought I was Hannibal Lecter the way they treated me. By the time one of the guys shouted 'Clear' for the doctor to enter the room I was tied upside down wriggling like a worm, screaming every swear word I could think of. Looking back I must have looked as mad as a hatter.

The doctor knelt down about four feet away and turning his head upside down said.

'Is there anything you'd like to tell me Russell?'

'Yeah' I replied 'go fuck yourself.'

For that I was shaken violently. Still shouting for them to let me go, the doctor nodded at the door and in walked a male nurse with my new jacket. I was screaming and screaming with anger. I was so mad, not at the staff but because I knew my brother and wife had told the doctors everything I'd done. I knew at that point there was no one I could talk to or trust.

'Get him on the bed and hold him down' said the doctor to the staff who were still holding me. He was passed a syringe. I kicked, swore, spat, you name it I did it, but there was no way I could fight off the three men. The next thing I knew I was laying face down on my bed with two of the men kneeling on my back, being injected by the doctor. When I later woke up I saw that my room had been turned upside down and the nurses were now putting everything back for me. Sitting up I noticed one of the guys from earlier was standing at the bottom of my bed.

'Are you going to be good now?' he asked.

Like a little naughty boy, I just nodded at him. One nurse told him it was OK for him to stand outside my room, while the other nurses explained that from now on I would have to take all my medication in front of the staff, and they meant all the medication I had previously been on.

'Do you understand?' she asked.

I just nodded.

She went on, 'Every night at nine I'll come to you with your medication, but we will not leave Russell, until we are happy that you have swallowed all your tablets, do you understand me?'

Again I just nodded.

After she'd gone I just sat there crying for what seemed like hours. I thought to myself that I was never going to get out of there now. What made it worse was they were making me look mad, and I was beginning to feel mad. I no longer felt I had anyone I could talk to, no one I could share my fears with, no one but myself.

I was told I couldn't have any visitors for a week because of what I'd done. I missed my family but at the same time I felt so angry with them. Looking back I believe they thought they were doing what they thought was right, but I was the only one that knew I was feeling so much better for not taking all that medication. The doctors had said that my medication should be started up again with immediate effect.

'Open up Russell, I have to see if you have swallowed them all' said the nurse.

Standing there with my mouth wide open she said 'Good boy, I'll see you tomorrow night.'

What could I do? I had to swallow them. By the time I was forced to start taking my medication again it had been a fortnight since I had woken in the night and been found anywhere apart from my own bedroom. I remember it was the fifth night of being back on the drugs that I woke up in the back of a man's car (he did work for the hospital) and the coat I was wearing wasn't mine.

'It's OK Russell I'm taking you back, we all wondered where you had gone to' said the man.

'Where was I?' I asked.

'Oh only a few hundred yards away don't worry you'll be back in bed in no time'

As I climbed back into my bed I knew I had been right all along. It was getting the doctors to believe me that mattered, but maybe it would be better not to even try.

I knew I had to stop taking my tablets but how could I if everyone kept looking into my mouth?

I realised I had no choice but to make myself sick. Every night after I had taken my medication I'd stand like a good boy and open my mouth just to show I'd swallowed what ever they had given me, then I'd go into the bathroom and make myself sick.

I hated doing it but I knew there was nothing more I could do. It worked and I stopped walking at night. The down side was because I was taking all my medication at the same time my fits started to come back, and fast. There was nothing I could do apart from retrieve my epilepsy tablets which I hated doing, but I had no other choice. From then on after I'd been sick in the sink, I'd pick my epilepsy tablets out, give them a quick swill and get them down again as quickly as possible before I really was sick.

When I was allowed to have visitors I was that glad to see them I didn't go on too much about what they had done, but I knew this time I wasn't going to tell a soul about what I was doing. My chats with Mr Jones continued; even though I felt I could trust him I knew in my heart that if my brother and wife had told on me then he surely would. Mr Jones still advised me to tell those close to me that I was gay, but I felt I wasn't ready to do this.

'You don't have anything to lose Russell, you have already lost everything you've had' he would say. (Mmm, thanks for reminding me)

Who do I tell first, my wife my brother or my father? I couldn't, not yet; I needed to get myself well first and out of the hospital.

The weekly meetings with the doctors were going well; if they had told me to jump I'd have asked 'how high?' At one of the meetings a doctor noticed how much weight I'd lost and asked how I was getting my food, as he knew I wasn't going to the main dinner hall. I assured him I was feeling OK and that my family were bringing my food in for me. He was happy with this answer.

I remember looking out of my window and watching a robin flying around the hospital grounds, thinking how happy he looked and how he was free to just fly off to anywhere he wanted to go, how lucky he was. Just then there was a knock at my bedroom door. It was a nurse, who on entering asked me to get ready for a meeting that was being held that day. I had an hour to get ready and meet her at her office. I wondered why they hadn't told me the previous day or even days before about the meeting; they had always done so in the past. This worried me and the more I thought about it the more I thought they were going to do something, but what I didn't know.

As I walked into the room I was shocked to see my brother, father and wife. It made me feel sick; each one of them got up to meet me but I couldn't speak; a nervous smile was all I could bring myself to give. As well as Mr Jones there were a few other doctors in the room and I recognised the social worker from last time, the one that told me I wasn't allowed to go home. Still unsure why I was there I sat myself down. Mr Jones was invited to start the meeting and as he started talking about me I remember thinking 'Oh shit, he's going to tell them all I'm mad and worse of all that I'm gay', but he didn't; Instead he told them how well I'd been doing and how in his opinion I was OK to leave the hospital.

I couldn't believe what I'd just heard, was it a joke? Why was I there? Why was he saying I could go home? Was he just seeing how I would react? Were they all there to see how I would react? I was too scared to speak, never mind move. Mr Jones went on to say he still wanted to meet with me every week which again meant it wouldn't be possible for me to move in with my father or brother. I was also told that I would still be too much work for my wife because of her looking after the children on her own.

All the doctors agreed that if I could find somewhere to live I would be allowed to leave. A lot of the people in the hospital were allowed out for the day but they had to be back in before tea. My father asked if it was OK for him to take me out for the day because I'd not been out of the hospital for such a long time. This was agreed. I felt numb, everyone had said everything I wanted to hear; I wanted to scream with joy but didn't, it was best to sit quietly, I thought.

Mr Jones said he would help me to find somewhere to live and a meeting was arranged for one week later. Thank God! I was getting somewhere at long last. I just had to keep it quiet from every one that I was still making myself sick every time I took my medication.

You'll Never Make a Hairdresser

'Is there anything you'd like to say Russell?' asked Mr Jones.

I didn't want to rock the boat, I was too scared I might say something that would result in them keeping me there even longer, so I said 'No'

As my father was leaving I asked if he could take me somewhere.

'Yes, where do you want to go, maybe for a nice meal?'

'No I'd like you to take me to the local paper shop so I can get a newspaper' I said.

'But you have the chance to go anywhere you want, you just want me to pop you around the corner to get you a newspaper, why?' Dad asked.

'You were in the meeting Dad. As soon as I find somewhere to live I can get out of here, I'm going to find a flat before they change their minds.'

'Oh there's enough time for that Russell, what's the rush?'

'Dad, just take me to the bloody paper shop'

After reading through the local paper I started to ring about the flats that I'd seen advertised. To start with the flats were vacant, but as soon as I told them my situation and where I was coming from they had suddenly gone. There were two things letting me down; one was that I had no deposit and the second was that I had told them where I was staying at that moment; big mistake. One day Mr Jones came to see me.

'Get your coat on, I believe I've found you a flat.'

I ran out of that hospital as quick as I could and jumped into his car. We pulled up outside a large house which looked to me as if it was just about to fall down. There were black bin bags stuck to windows like curtains, the gardens were full of old beds and car parts and there was that much rubbish outside we could hardly get to the main door. I couldn't believe that he had brought me here.

'Come on, let's have a look inside' he said with a big smile on his face.

As we walked in the main door there must have been twenty or thirty bin bags full of rubbish, and the smell was so strong it made me feel sick. The tears started to roll down my face.

'What's wrong, why are you crying?' he asked.

'Did you ever see where I lived with my wife and children?' I asked.

'Yes, but you have nowhere to live Russell' he replied.

'My children will have to come and visit me wherever I decide to live, and I can tell you now there is no way I would allow them to come here and see their dad living in a place like this' I said.

'But as I have said Russell, you have nowhere to live, is this not better than them seeing their father in a hospital?'

'No Mr Jones it's not, now please take me back'

I never went inside the flat, I got back into the car and waited until Mr Jones came back. Driving back to the hospital Mr Jones said.

'You have to forget where you came from Russell, and you won't get any better than that.'

'If that's what you offer people who have just come out of this hospital then God fucking help them; I'd rather be dead than live there and have my own kids come to see me there' I said.

'Well, you see if you can find a better place then.'

'Oh I will' I replied.

I soon found a very nice flat. My father and brother gave me the deposit and even though I was on sickness benefit the owner allowed me to rent it. The fits were still happening, but not as often as they had been, and as long as the sleep walking stayed away I felt I could live with them; I also knew I wouldn't have to make myself sick any more. The day I moved into my own flat I was so happy, yet at the same time sad and nervous. Happy because I was leaving that hospital behind me, but sad because I wasn't going home to my wife and children and nervous because I hadn't lived on my own for years. Now here I was moving into my own home with just the few clothes that I stood up in and of course, Mr Epilepsy.

I was living in a flat on just thirty six pounds a week sickness benefit. No job, no telephone, no friends and no family around me. Apart from my father and brother coming from Manchester to see me there was no one else. The children would come and visit me as often as their mother could bring them, but with money tight for her as well, it wasn't that often and with no car I could never get to see them. The flat I was staying in was right by the sea, it was such a beautiful place to live, yet after a few weeks I started feeling lonely. I was too nervous to go out in case I had a fit. Looking back I remember being so scared at the thought of having to go out anywhere, but I knew I had to. After sitting in the flat for months I gradually started walking around the block, as I got more confident I would go that bit further and so on.

Once I'd found the sea I used to sit there all day just people watching; watching the boats coming back from their fishing trips and all the kids playing in the sand. That was fine for a while but I soon missed my old life, the life I used to have. I was still having my meetings with Mr Jones but all we talked about was how and when I was going to come out, and tell the people close to me that I was gay. He believed I would feel much better when it was all out in the open, however I was not so sure.

I know I was living alone, but apart from not having a pot to piss in I still had my brother, father, kids and my wife. If I tell them now, I thought, I'll lose them as well. Looking back, I question whether I was being selfish or was I that desperate that I still wanted them all in my life, and I didn't want to lose anyone else again? Whatever it was I was thinking, putting it off was only making life hell for all involved. I was sure I'd never see my father again, and I wasn't sure how my brother would take it; but one thing I knew for sure my wife would definitely not stay around, and why should she?

How could I tell her? She had done nothing wrong, but then again had I? Was it wrong of me to have married the woman I loved?

Whatever people may think, I would never change that time in my life. I loved my wife, I had a wonderful life with her and together we had two beautiful children. She was 29 and I believe it was unfair of me to try and hold on to my best friend for any longer. I say 'best friend' because that's what my wife had become, and the last thing I wanted to do was hurt her. It was time that the truth came out.

Now I had to decide who to tell first and when to tell them. My wife I hear you shout, but again I didn't want to lose the only woman apart from my sister who I had ever loved, and selfishly I didn't want to lose my best friend. I would talk and talk to Mr Jones and although he was the one that had prompted me to tell my family, a date was never agreed. Time just seemed to go on and on. I remember one night going for a walk on the local beach, it had starting to go dark. I thought I'd use the pay phone and see what the kids were up to and see how my wife was. I didn't plan it, it just came out. My wife was talking, going on about the day to day running of her home when it just came out.

'I'm gay' I said. The rest they say is history, and the rest of that conversation will stay with me and my ex-wife forever.

The next time I saw my brother I told him about my being gay. I shouldn't have been surprised about the amount of support he gave me and how understanding he was and still is. I could never repay what my brother has done for me, and for this I thank him with all my heart.

My father was also OK with the news I was gay. I believe he thought it was connected to my epilepsy. He later told one of my boyfriends, 'I wouldn't get too comfy mate, when his tablets kick in he'll drop you like a ton of bricks and go back to his wife.' This always makes me laugh. The rest of the family did hear but offered no support. The next time I saw Mr Jones he was shocked that I had told everyone, but believed I had done the right thing. Only time would tell.

You'll Never Make a Hairdresser

Caravan

The flat I was living in was nice but it was on the second floor of a house. On the days I felt I couldn't go out, and there were quite a few, I found myself just sitting in the bay of the window looking down on the heads of the passers by; not very exciting. I needed to move, but where to I didn't know. I wasn't ready to go back to work, but at the same time I knew I needed money, or at least my family did. For someone who had previously had his own salon I no longer owned a hair pin let alone a pair of scissors. Word soon got around that I was a hairdresser, and even the people who didn't know me wanted their hair cut. I could have been anyone or done anything; it's amazing what people will put up with, just to get things on the cheap. When my father called one day I asked him if he would loan me some money so I could get myself a few hairdressing items that I needed to start up again. I had always bought my scissors like all hairdressers from the hairdressing warehouse, but I knew I could never pay their prices right now, so Boots own just had to do.

I remember paying a fiver for the scissors and thinking how shit they would be; but to my surprise they did the job and I must say they were actually quite good. I would have laughed my head off if I'd known any of my staff had paid a fiver for a pair of scissors from Boots, but beggars could not be choosers. With my cheap scissors in hand I was ready to start my hairdressing career all over again.

The trouble with living by the sea was that most of the people living there were OAPs and all they wanted were dry cuts or shampoo and sets, and none of them wanted to pay more than two quid at the most. My hairdressing round grew quickly, which meant I was walking more and more and not getting very far. Blow this I thought, they can start coming to me, I'm not walking my arse off for two quid. I thought that by asking them to come to me I'd lose quite a few of the OAPs and this would leave more room for the younger ones to come around for their hair cut. However, within months I was running up and down the stairs of my flat letting in one O A P after the other; sometimes there were so many of them there they were making their own teas and coffees. Good job Spar was over the road, the amount of milk we used I should have got my own live-in cow.

Some of the ladies would empty my washer for me and even start my ironing. Sometimes I thought most of them didn't need their hair cut but just wanted to meet up with their mates. Whatever their reason for visiting the two quids soon mounted up and I was able to buy all the hairdressing things that I needed.

Every now and then I would do a daughter or son of one of the older ladies. This always brought me more younger ladies and gents, which meant in the long run I could charge more money. Even though I didn't like the flat that much it was starting to look nice, but I was still on the look out for a move, especially because some of the older ladies had started to moan about the stairs. 'they're too steep for me; I'm finding it harder and harder every time I come' they would say.

One of my older ladies asked me if I could go and do her sister's hair. She couldn't come over to my flat because she wasn't very well. At first I didn't want to go but I'm so glad I did.

'Once you've passed the roundabout turn left, go over the train track and the camp site is on the right, next to the local tip' said the sister.

'Where?' I thought. No wonder she wasn't well, it sounded like she was living in a right dump. I was shocked when I got there, the caravan site she lived on was so nice. Most of the caravans were owned, but I later found out that some of the owners rented their vans out on long lets. Each caravan came with its own small garden; I couldn't believe how similar they were to a small bungalow. They had their own telephone lines and post boxes with their names on. It was so quiet there, I loved it. I'd made up my mind I wanted one. After doing the woman's hair I asked her all about the caravan site and how I might be able to rent one. With my two quid and all the information I needed I was off. There were only about fifty vans on the site and most, if not all, belonged to the elderly. This was the right place for me; having no car, I could have my own hairdressing round right on my own door step.

I was only seeing Mr Jones once a month now and most of that time I felt I was listening to him more than he was to me. I had started to think enough is enough. I was still trying to stay in touch with my ex wife so I could see the children but things were still a bit raw so their visits were still sporadic. I was still fitting, but luckily I was slowly learning to cope with the fits better day by day. I could now tell when they were about to happen. That's a good thing I was told, but often knowing it was about to happen was just as bad as it happening. The fear of waiting was bad enough, then you had the fit to deal with. Sounds silly I know, but I would often get a nasty taste in my mouth. I soon learnt that the bad taste was my warning.

Everyone thought I was going mad when I told them I was moving into a caravan. I on the other hand thought it was great and couldn't wait to move. The caravan I was offered had one large bedroom, an open plan sitting room and kitchen. The kitchen was small but had everything I needed, and if anything was in some ways much better than the flat. I even had French doors that opened onto my own small garden; I loved it. I must have, as I ended up staying there seven years and still to this day I miss it so much and miss the friends I made there. If Johnny would agree to it I'd move into a new caravan tomorrow, it must be the gypsy in me.

It didn't take me long to adjust to life on the site and just as I thought I was getting busier than ever doing hair. I really wanted to go back to working in a salon but knew I was still not ready, and anyway who'd want me? No one knew me in North Wales as all the salons I'd worked in had been in Manchester. I knew if I moved back to Manchester and the fitting stopped I'd be able to walk into any salon and get a job, but I was so scared that if I did and continued to fit I'd be sacked; the risk was just too great at that moment. I couldn't take that chance, not just yet anyway. One of the guys that lived on the site was in his forties, he only worked part time because he'd had a heart problem. I got on so well with him and thanked god the day I met him. He knew so many people around the site, it was because of him and his contacts I was working morning till night. And then it happened. The caravan was full of people, two ladies were sat with colour on their hair, I was cutting another, one lady was doing my cleaning (Ha, I know, but I was busy) and another was waiting for her hair to be cut and had offered to start my ironing.

The knock at the door was so hard the caravan shook.

'I'll go love' said Pat 'you carry on doing Lyn's hair'

Pat was my cleaner, but she turned out be a good friend as well. She might not have had a pot to piss in but she would have given you the world if she had it. She cleaned two mornings a week; I did do as much as I could but with all the hairdressing I just couldn't fit it all in. A bit of cleaning meant Pat got free hair do's so she was happy and sometimes she even made meals for me. God, I missed her when she moved on.

'Bloody hell you look smart' said Pat as she opened the door 'have you come for your hair cut as well? Only there's a bloody queue'

'No I have not' replied the man 'I'm from the social security. Can I speak to Mr Hughes please?'

'Course you can love, come on in' said Pat.

Great, I thought, who's this?

'Mr Hughes I take it?' said the man as he stepped into the caravan.

'Yes, why who are you?' I asked.

'I have reason to believe you have been or are working illegally'

'Me' I said, stood in about a tonne of hair that lay on the floor, with Lyn sat in front of me having her hair cut.

'Yes you Mr Hughes, I can see you're very busy now doing your mobile hairdressing'
Before I could say an other word, Lyn whose hair I was cutting jumped up and said. 'Now wait one fucking minute Mr who ever you fucking are, I can assure you, this lad's not very well and there's no fucking way on this earth he's been working, how can he he's always here.'

'Well it looks to me madam' the man said 'that Mr Hughes is working whether he's ill or not.'

'You ask any of these ladies here mate' Lyn said. 'they'll all tell you the same as me, this boy cut's our hair now and then and in return we help out in his caravan.'

You'll Never Make a Hairdresser

'You should have come an hour earlier' shouted Joan from the other side of the caravan with full head colour on her hair. 'we were helping this poor lad up after he'd had one of his epileptic fits, isn't that right ladies?'

'Oh God yeah' said Sue coming from behind the ironing board. ' You go and tell who ever sent you here love, that not one penny passes hands here, like Lyn said we help him and in return he does our hair.'

In a way I felt sorry for the poor man stood there in the van full of all these ladies. One wrong word from him and I'm sure they would have pounced. There was no way they were going to let anything happen to me; they all needed me, but not as much as I needed them, well I did that day.

'So Mr Hughes' said the man 'you never take any money from these ladies?'

'No' I said.

'And you can't prove he does' shouts Pat.

'OK' he said 'I'll get back in touch with you when I have spoken to my supervisor'

'You do that love' said Lyn walking him to the caravan door. 'And if you're supervisor needs to talk to any of us, you just call us, do you hear me now?'

'I do and will, thank you all for your time, I'll be in touch'

'Well that was lucky love' said Lyn 'from now on you'll have to come to our vans, at least for the next few months anyway.'

I knew I was working but the few quid I got was well needed; my fags alone cost more than the sick money I was getting.
The next time I saw Mr Jones I told him all about the man from the Social Security that had called at the caravan. He believed it was good that I was trying to do some work, therapeutic work he called it and I agreed. Mr Jones said he would write to this man from the Social Security and tell him as long as no money was changing

hands then he believed I should carry on with the work I was doing as in his opinion it was a good way of helping me get back into work.

So for now everything seemed OK again. Like Mr Jones had said, the work I was doing was very therapeutic for me. The caravan was now rocking, the clients were also getting younger which meant I could charge more. All in all the move to the caravan had been the best move I'd made in a long time. I'd been living in the caravan for quite a while by the time the girls came around to see me. I thought the van was looking good, the sun was shining, I had nice food on the table and I felt I'd done all I could to make their visit good. But the girls didn't like it, they had never known anyone who lived in a caravan let alone their own father. As time moved on the girls were allowed to stay over now and then on a Saturday night, these were our fun nights, for the younger girls anyway.

Because there was only one bedroom in the caravan two of the girls would sleep in the bed and the rest of us would make a camp bed up on the living room floor. The kids liked this bit, as they would say it was like sleeping in a dolls' house. I felt that half of the time the girls hated the trips to their dad's caravan, but it was the only way we could see each other for now as I was still unable to drive.

The ladies all knew that when the girls came over I couldn't do their hair, and to be fair they were always good and never bothered me, apart from sending things over for the girls to play with or bringing the cakes they had baked for them to eat. I'd started to save up for a car, even though my driving licence had been taken away from me because of the fits. I knew that one day I'd get it back and when I did I wanted to have the money ready so I could go out and get a car. Whenever the girls came around to see me in the caravan there wasn't that much we could do without needing a car, but I hoped that would soon change; all I had to do was get well and get the money together to buy that car.

My father and brother came across a man in Manchester who sold anything and everything that had been left on trains; we called it the lost and found. They would go and put a bid to buy these things, the only downside being they didn't know what they were buying! All the items were kept in black bin bags and they weren't allowed to open the bags first, which meant they had to bid blind. I found it amazing and still do at the amount of things that people leave on trains and never bother to go back for. There would be anything from swimming things that a young girl had left to brand new clothes still bagged from Next. If they were successful in winning the bid then they were free to go home with the goods. There would be hundreds of pairs of glasses that were no good to anyone so Dad would take them somewhere that would send them to the third world countries. They would give items to dogs homes and charity shops; lots of good came out of this and I was so happy at what they did.

Some things did find their way up to me in North Wales, things that I didn't
necessary need or wouldn't use. I'd put them to one side because they were just too good to throw away. Then one day I asked my brother if he wanted to do a car boot sale with me, as I had that much stuff in North Wales it seemed silly holding on to it. As I didn't have a car I couldn't do the car boot alone. My brother loved the idea and he agreed to bring a lot more of the items he had at his own home. The car boots were a huge success. We made plenty of money and the laughs we shared with each other will stay with me for ever. It would have been too much for us both to do a car boot every week so we decided every fortnight was enough. My brother would stay over with me the night before, ready for an early start in the morning. It was hard work but we loved it. I wish I could do one with him now.

I believe everyone should do a car boot once in their life. It's one of those must do things before you die, ha! Every fortnight the items just kept coming up from Manchester and I believe at one point we had over a hundred umbrellas, over seventy walking sticks and mobile phones; you name it, we had it, and they ranged from the cheapest on the market to the most desirable designer model that was in at that time. Sometimes we didn't have the time to sort the bags out. Soon on those occasions the things ended up going in the pound box. Everything we had sold like hot cakes, and every time we did the car boot we always had plenty of people around our stall. It was funny with Tommy being the straight guy, who would just throw the items on the floor with me then displaying them at their best, but it worked so well. I remember one day I went for a walk after the rush had finished and I saw a stereo player on this man's stall for sale. He wanted twenty pounds. I asked him what the lowest price was that he would take. 'Fifteen pounds' he said, so I paid him.

'We're here to sell, not buy' said Tommy when I got back with my find. 'We have enough crap' he went on.

I got in the back of the car with the stereo and out came my polish. I knew this stereo was worth more than fifteen pounds and It came up like new by the time I'd finished cleaning it. And so a sixty pound sticker went on it.

'You'll never get sixty quid for that' said Tommy.

'I know, but you watch, I'll get fifty' I replied.

It wasn't long before I saw the original seller coming over to our stall shouting 'Hey you little bastard, that stereo was mine.'

Tommy jumped up from his chair asking me 'I thought you'd bought it?'

'I did' I said trying to get out of this man's way.

Tommy walked over to meet the man and as he got closer I heard Tommy saying 'Well mate what's your fucking problem?'

'I'll tell you what my fucking problem is, that little twat (pointing at me) only paid me fifteen quid for that stereo and now he's selling it for fucking sixty'

'Did you get you're fifteen quid ?' Tommy shouted back to the man, who was by now leaning over our stall ready to grab me. Tommy shouted even louder. 'Did you get you're fifteen quid?'

'Yeah' the man shouted back.

'Well that's all you wanted' Tommy said. 'Now get the fuck away from this stall before you get the fucking stereo over your head'. I was so glad the man walked off. Turning around to me Tommy said

'You'd better fucking sell that stereo now after all that'. I did sell it that day, and I did get the fifty pounds I wanted.

We got to know the other guys who had been doing the car boots for years, and in time they would always wait until Tommy and I arrived so that they could pitch up next to us, because they knew that we always attracted the crowds. I shall never forget the time Tommy and I had stayed up late the night before a car boot having a few drinks. On the Sunday Tommy woke up with a really bad head. He kept asking for some headache tablets which I didn't have, so to shut him up, I gave him some of my epilepsy tablets. I thought, well these are for my head and so they will help him too. I didn't tell him what they were as I watched him take them.

The next thing I remember is us driving down the road and Tommy saying 'God, I don't feel well.'

'Oh you'll be OK when we get there' I replied.

As we pulled up there were loads of people waiting to see what kind of items we had for sale.

'Come on Tom' I said getting out of the car.
'I can't I think, I'm dying' he replied. Not thinking anything I just laughed it off.

As the car came to a stop I couldn't see out of our windows because of the number of people who were trying to look inside the car to see what we had brought. All the time poor Tommy kept saying 'I have to get the fuck out of here'. It was madness. I turned to Tommy and said 'There is no way I'm going to leave now we're here and all these people want to give us money for all this crap'

There was no time for doing my display so I just threw the things on the floor and let everyone grab what they wanted. I looked around to see poor Tommy crawling from the front seat onto the back. He just curled up like a baby and stayed there. I was making us a bomb, but every time I had the to chance I'd looked in and ask how he was.

'I'm fucking shaking like a leaf' he said.

How could I tell him that it was me who had given him the wrong tablets?! I didn't know he would react like that, did I? After another very successful day we went back home to the caravan. Tommy was only supposed to stay one night (Saturday) then go home after the car boot, but because he still felt so ill he stayed the Sunday night as well. Poor Tom, I felt so sorry for him and guilty too, but I never did tell him about the tablets I'd given to him. He'll know now and Tommy I'm so very sorry, you know I love you!

Over the months the car boot was doing that well the items from the lost and found were not coming in fast enough, we needed more and more things to sell. One of the old dears whose hair I'd been doing in the week had told me that her husband went to an auction every Wednesday in Llandudno.

'I believe you'll get loads of things from there to sell' she said.

So off I went. When I got there I loved it, even though it was in a dirty old building at the back of town with just one toilet for everyone to use, and a sweaty old butty bar in the corner. I'd never seen anything like it before but knew I would end up going every week. I will always remember my father saying 'Where there's shit there's money', and there was certainly a lot of shit around that auction. If shit did make money I'd go every day if I had to.

I was surprised just how many of the other car booters were there buying so much crap; no wonder they were never busy, because they never bought anything that was of any quality. Now I'd found the auction and knew I too could sell some of the items the other men had been selling I just had to find a way of getting them home to my caravan, as I'd had to get the bus into town. I remembered the old lady from the caravan park who said her husband went every Wednesday, so I got in touch with him and he agreed that for a small fee he would bring back any items I bought and give me a lift to the auction as well. Allan had a large van so there was no limit to the amount of things I could buy.

During this time I was still having the odd fit, but not half as many as I had previously been having. I continued to see Mr Jones and we still chatted about my past and my sister Allyson, but I still felt the more I spoke with him the more depressed I was feeling. My hairdressing in the caravan was getting out of control, and thank god it was, it was times like that that I was thankful I had hairdressing because it gave me some money to live on.

One day there was a knock at my door. I opened it to a woman who introduced herself as a hairdresser who had her own salon just around the corner from the caravan site I was living on. After I asked her in, she went on to explain that a lot of her clientele were now coming to my caravan to have their hair cut. She asked me if I'd consider going to work for her. I explained my situation and said that I was on sickness benefit because of my epilepsy; and how one day I could be well for work but not the next. I would have loved the job but I knew I was not ready. We agreed to stay in touch and I said I'd let her know when I felt I'd be ready for work again.

I had already been thinking about going back to work before she had come to see me, but before I'd met her I didn't know where I was going to go for a new job; every salon I'd seen in the town seemed so old fashioned compared to where I'd worked before. Mr Jones' words came back to haunt me (beggars cannot be choosers) and I realised I had to start somewhere. Maybe this woman was my answer after all. Only time would tell.

I should have known by the way she was dressed when she came to see me as to what kind of salon she would be running, but nevertheless it still shocked me the first time I walked in. The waiting area had an old couch that looked like it had just been dragged out of someone's house and the table in front of me stood covered in old newspapers trying to hide the big crack in the glass top. There was hair everywhere I looked, and the back window was covered with a net curtain that sagged in the middle. I felt like I'd just stepped back in time and was sitting in Mr Quinn's salon back in Wythenshawe. I was shocked when I was asked to do a cut and blow, just so she could see if I was good enough to work in her salon; was taking all her clients not proof enough of my ability to cut hair? I already knew then this wasn't the salon for me, but I didn't want to hurt her feelings so I agreed to do the cut and blow. She watched every move I made and at the end of my cut and blow I was told I had the job; what a surprise! The only way I could get out of there was to decline the salary she was offering and thank god she said she'd have to think about the new wage I had asked for.

'I'll be in touch' she said as I left. I never heard from her again. Nice lady, wrong salon.

What I did find in this ladies' salon was myself again. I liked being in a salon; I liked being stood behind the chair and I liked the fact that she liked my work. I felt ready to go back to what I loved doing most of all, hairdressing in a nice salon. I knew I wasn't going to find Market Street, Manchester in Llandudno, but hoped I'd find somewhere with a bit of class. After looking around I went into what I thought at the time to be the best salon in town. They weren't advertising for staff but I thought if I walked in and told them I was a stylist that had just moved up from Manchester they might just give me the break I was looking for. The young lady behind the desk asked me to take a seat while she went and got the salon manager. When he came I tried to explain in brief what work I had done before and why I only wanted part time work at that moment.

'I noticed you haven't brought any of your hairdressing tools with you. If I loan you some of ours do you think you would be able to do a cut for us or maybe a cut and blow now so I can see your work?' he asked.

'Yes sure, I'd love to' I replied

Walking on that salon floor I felt like an actor walking on stage. As soon as I was out there I loved it. All the pain I'd suffered over the last few years had suddenly gone away. I was there cutting, chatting, laughing, I felt I was back. After cutting the ladies' hair I was asked to wait in the reception while the manager went to talk to the main stylist. As he got closer he gave me a big smile. I knew then I had a job. He went on to explain that although the salon was not looking for another stylist they were prepared to offer me a part time position. I was so happy I couldn't wait to get home and call my brother and father. They were both thrilled too, but told me to go easy and not to overdo it. If anything I believed working in the salon would be far easier than working from the caravan, as in the caravan I was doing all the hair washing etc. The date was set for me to start my job, so off I went to the social to tell them that I was going to start work part time. I remember I was there for hours filling in the forms just to get help with my rent and rates until I worked full time, when I would be able to pay my own way in life again. All that was sorted and I was ready. I was so desperate to get my life back; I knew I was doing well with all the hairdressing I was doing at the caravan and with the car boot money coming in, but it was not a life I wanted. Yes it was funny, but to me it was not real. I missed working with younger people, with other hairstylists and with the public.

I'd not heard from any of my sisters or my stepmother for years, but they all knew what I was up to; it was always getting back to them via dad. That's what happens when you're in touch with one member of your family and they're in touch with everyone else. I had nothing to hide, if anything I hoped they could see I was trying to get on with my life instead of sitting in some hole and crying about what I should have had. I was shocked one night when I answered my phone to one of the family who I had not spoken to for years. It was strange hearing their voice. To my surprise they went on to say that they had heard that I was thinking of going back to work. 'Yes' I said with joy in my voice. 'You silly, silly bastard, I thought you were a clever guy, but now I know you're thick as shit' was their reply. Although I was shocked I went on to ask 'Why?' 'Because you have a sickness book there that gives you thirty seven pounds a week and you'll never have to work a fucking day in your life again. If you give that up then you must be thick'.

I couldn't believe what I was hearing; as always I was very polite and got them off the phone as quickly as I could. How could anyone think that having a sickness book with thirty seven pounds a week in it was enough to live on for the rest of their life, and why would I want to sit around at home and do nothing? Once I'd put the phone down I sat there in my caravan and cried. Why had that person called me after all those years if that was all they had wanted to say? I couldn't then and never will understand why that person had said those things to me; what did hit me that night, and I believe it was the reason why I was so upset, was the realisation my family and I were worlds apart. A few years later the same person called back. We'd never spoken since the last time they told me I was thick as shit. They called to tell me their house phone was being cut off because they couldn't afford to pay the bill and asked if I would loan them the money. Of course I said I was very sorry but I couldn't help them. I knew I could have paid their bill ten times over but why should I?. Before the phone went down abruptly I was told 'I fucking knew you'd say that, you fucking twat.' Maybe they understand now why I went back to work and how important it is to finance yourself. Saying that, I don't believe for one minute some people will ever understand.

I loved my new job. I found the way they did some things in the salon strange, but they soon picked up my way of doing things which they admitted were a better and easier way of making the salon a lot more money. When I started at the salon they were still using the cap to put hi or lo lights in peoples hair and they'd never used foil before. They'd seen it but had never tried it; all that changed when I got there and they all admitted the change was for the better. Within weeks my Thursday, Friday and Saturday column were busy and this meant everyone was happy.

I used to have to walk to the bus stop to catch my bus for work and in doing so I'd pass the same garage on my way. Every day I'd look at the cars and see which new ones were on display; not that I could buy one, because I still didn't have my driving licence back, but that didn't stop me from looking and saving. Although I was very grateful that all the older ladies had helped me in the past, I was finding it harder and harder to find the time to do their hair when I got home from work. For some time I would finish my day in the salon and then work most nights at the caravan just to get all the old dears done, and I was starting to get tired.

Walking for my bus one morning I had a banging headache. I was going to turn back and go home but then I knew I needed the money. Still walking, I hoped the pain would go away. I'd been in work for a few hours when one of the young girls came up to me and told me that my next lady was sat in the reception, she was having a her hair coloured that day. I asked the young girl if she would get my lady seated and gowned and I'd be over as soon as I could. With my head still banging I went to the toilet to wash my face, hoping I would feel a little better. However, by the time I'd got over to my next lady I knew that I still didn't feel right as I was chatting to her about her colour. Once she was happy and we'd both decided on what colour she was having I went off to mix it. I remember her smiling as I walked back to her with the tint bowls in hand, and that's all I remember. The fits were back.

When I came around the ambulance men were already there. As I sat up I noticed that every client had been moved from that part of the salon and all the other hairdressers were working pushed together at the other end. The poor woman that I was going to do couldn't be seen. To this day I still don't know what happened to her or if she ever did get her hair done. I hope she did. Because of the state I was in I was taken back to the local hospital again. I knew what was coming; I'd been through it all before. I was told I'd have to stay in hospital overnight and that my father was going to come and collect me the next day to take me home. I had no things with me, and because of the fit my pants were now on the radiator beside me trying to dry out. Some people pee themselves when they have a fit, or soil themselves, I was lucky that day that I'd only peed. I was shocked to see my salon manager walking towards me on the ward, and was thinking how nice it was of him to come and see me. I noticed he'd had brought my hairdressing tools with him. 'Thanks for coming' I said 'you should have left them at the salon for me'. 'I'm so sorry Russell' he said 'but because of what has happened today I feel you cannot come back to work' 'Why' I said 'this is only a one off, I swear it won't happen again' 'You can't guarantee that Russell, but when you feel better do call back into the salon and we'll see what, if anything we can do, again I'm so very sorry' he said as he walked away. It sounds silly now but I just lay there crying.

I wanted that job. I was enjoying it there and thought I would have been there for years. Looking back I realise now that the salon could have been prosecuted for the way they ended my employment but still I did nothing about it. Dad picked me up the very next day and took me home to the caravan. I remember he had brought lots of shopping with him for me. He had dropped it all off at the caravan on his way to pick me up from the hospital, bless. Now it was back to Mr Jones and back to the social security for more help. There was nothing I could do. I was lucky that I still had my old dears to fall back on, and only a few days before I was getting ready to call it a day with all of them all; thank God I didn't. So it was back to working in the caravan and going to the auction on a Wednesday, play life as I would call it. Arriving at the auction one Wednesday I remember looking over the other side of the room and seeing a very handsome looking guy. Every time I looked over he was looking back in my direction and I wondered if he was gay. To be fair he didn't look it, and there was no way I was going to go straight up to him and ask. That week I got my things together that I had bought and left with Allan.

The following week Mr handsome was there again. This time he smiled. I remember thinking Oh my god! and feeling all butterflies inside me. But why? I didn't know the answer because in my mind I was sure he was straight. That Sunday when Tommy and I were doing the car boot I was tidying up our stall trying to make it look all nice when I heard Tommy say 'You all right mate?' 'Fine thank you' the man replied. I looked up and there was Mr handsome stood at my stall. I nearly fell over. He was looking at the items we had for sale on the table, then as he walked away he turned around and smiled. The butterflies were back. 'Do you know him?' Tommy asked. 'No' I said smiling 'but I've got a feeling I will do soon.' I couldn't wait to get back to the auction that week. Poor Allan was talking away as he drove and I wasn't listening to a word he was saying, all I could do was stare out of the windows thinking of Mr handsome. Half way through the day the auction would close for lunch. Allan and I would always go home because it was only up the road from where we lived, plus neither of us could afford to go out for lunch.

I was just about to walk out of the auction when Mr handsome stood right in front of me. 'Hello' he said 'My name is Steve'. 'Oh Hi' I said looking startled 'My name's Russell'. 'Well it's nice to meet you Russell' Steve said, sticking out his hand towards me. 'Nice to meet you too Steve' I replied, taking his hand. I thought I was going to drop down dead right there on the spot. As we shook hands he stared right into my eyes. 'What are you doing now?' Steve asked. Before I could answer he said 'I was wondering if you'd like to have a wet lunch with me?' By now Allan was standing right at my side. I couldn't believe what Steve had just asked me. 'What!' I shouted back at him 'No I most certainly do not want a wet lunch with you' Me and Allan walked off leaving Steve stood there. 'I'm so sorry about that Allan' I said as we were climbing into his van. 'I have no idea why that man would ask me that'. Allan started laughing then said 'Do you know what he was asking you?' 'I can only imagine it was something sexual' I said back. Still laughing Allan said 'He was only asking you if you wanted to go for a pint (wet lunch) with him'. I couldn't believe it, I must have looked so stupid to Steve. 'Oh well, fuck it' I said, feeling so embarrassed. 'He won't ask me again'.

Walking back into the auction after lunch I couldn't see Steve but knew he would be somewhere in the building. I didn't dare look around in case he saw me looking; still feeling embarrassed, Allan and I just headed towards the front as there were quite a lot of items we wanted that day. One was a wooden bar stool that I'd spotted earlier in the morning which I thought would come in handy when the kids came around. After a while it was time to start the bidding on the wooden bar stool. I already had a sum in mind of how much I'd be prepared to pay, and I knew fifteen pounds was my lot for it, but hopefully no one else wanted it so I could get it for less than a fiver. The bidding started at three pounds fifty. I raised my hand. 'four fifty' the auctioneer shouted, then in quick succession he went on, 'Five fifty, six fifty, seven fifty, eight fifty' he looked back at me and I nodded my head again. 'Nine fifty here in the front' the auctioneer shouted to the rest of the room. Then he shouted 'Ten fifty, eleven fifty' looking back at me I nodded again. By this time I was wishing that whoever was bidding at the back of me would just piss off and let me have the stool.

'I have thirteen fifty at the back of the room' the auctioneer said looking right at me. Was I willing to go one more? I nodded. 'Fourteen fifty in the front sir' the auctioneer said looking at the back of the room. I was dying to turn around to see who was out bidding me but didn't. Just then the auctioneer looked back at me saying. 'Your bid sir; we're on fifteen fifty, I've never known a wooden stool draw so much attention' Fifteen fifty? I was willing to go to fifteen pounds, should I go one more? Best not I thought, I could be here all day, I shook my head to the auctioneer. 'Fifteen fifty it is then, what's your number, sir?' the auctioneer shouted to the man who had just bought the wooden stool.

'Are you ready to go now?' asks Allan. Still feeling disappointed about the wooden stool I said. 'Yeah, lets go' Walking back to Allan's van I heard a man's voice shout 'What about your stool?' Turning around I saw Steve running towards us. 'So it was you bidding against me?' I asked Steve with a smile. 'Yeah I'm afraid so, now do you want this bloody stool or not?' Steve said offering me the stool. 'But I thought you wanted it' I replied. 'I only bid for it because I knew you wanted it' Steve said. 'But why?' I asked.

'Just take the bleeding stool and tell him you'll go for a wet lunch with him' said Allan, 'I'm freezing stood here' 'Is that what you'd like?' I asked, turning to Steve. 'Very much so Russell' he replied. After exchanging telephone numbers I agreed to call Steve, then walked off with Allan towards his van, with the stool in hand.

'I bet you're happy you got your stool aren't you?' Allan said as we both climbed into his van. 'No, I'm more happy I've got his phone number' I replied. Poor Allan; if he didn't know I was gay then he did now. Steve called me that night but I was working on the old ladies so we didn't have long to talk. I told him I was glad that he'd called and I would call him back the next day. It was a strange feeling; yes I knew I was gay but in the past I'd have met a guy, we'd do whatever we wanted, usually there and then, and afterwards probably never meet each other again. Not a nice way to go through life I know, but that's how it is for a lot of gay men, whether you liked it or not that's how gay life was. Steve felt different; to me he seemed so straight, what more could a gay guy want; I had my very own straight/gay man. I soon found out just how different Steve was from all the other men I'd met.

I was still seeing Mr Jones. God, how my life was turning out right in front of his eyes. By now we were laughing at things that were happening to me. I'm sure he couldn't wait to meet up with me just to get an up date.

Steve and I arranged to go for that wet lunch on the following Wednesday, so it looked like Allan was going home on his own for his lunch! Arriving at the auction Steve came over and stood with Allan and me. Steve was even running over the road to get our cups of teas and Allan was very impressed, as was I. A good morning was had by all and as it was time for Allan to head off home for his lunch we agreed to meet up with him later. As for me, I still didn't know if Steve was the same as all the other guys I'd met and his wet lunch wasn't a drink in the pub but a quick shag behind it instead. Whatever it was though I was right up for it regardless. 'There's a nice pub just around the corner' Steve said as we walked from the auction room. It was at this point I questioned whether I was actually disappointed that we weren't doing the usual quick shag thing, but whatever Steve had in mind I was happy to go along with it. We got our drinks and sat down. I soon realised this was the first time I'd ever sat in a bar with another gay man. It felt so strange.

As Steve started to talk I couldn't quite believe what he was saying. He went on to explain that he quickly realised I was gay. He told me that he wasn't gay, never had been and up until the day he'd met me he never wanted to or even thought about it. I sat there shocked, thinking I fucking knew you weren't gay. The only thing I was waiting for now was for him to lean over the table and smack me in the face, but he didn't. He went on to say he was married and that his wife has just had their second baby. By this time I just sat there stunned. 'Even before I had spoken to you I was at home thinking about you all the time, and now I have you here I don't know quite what to say or do' Steve said. My heart sank; not only had the chance of a quick shag gone that day, but now it looked like I'd never be getting it.

I continued to listen to Steve talking, still not knowing what to say. If anything when Steve asked me what I thought all I wanted to do was leave, but I didn't. He went on to question me about how I'd known I was gay, when had I realised and how old I'd been when I first slept with a man?.

I told him I didn't want to answer any of his questions, why should I?, it wouldn't get me anywhere. The time came for us to leave as Allan would be back waiting for us in the auction.
'I want to go back now, and I think it will be best for us both if we don't see each other again'. 'Oh no please don't say that, why are you saying that?' Steve asked. 'Steve you've just sat right in front of me and told me that you think you like me, you're not gay and that your wife has just had your second baby. You ask yourself why I think it's best if we don't see each other again'. We walked out of the pub and back to the auction in silence, then just before I walked into the auction room Steve said 'Can I ask you something and please tell me the truth?' I didn't want to look at him, I felt scared 'Yes, ask me' 'Do you think I'm an attractive man?' 'Yes Steve, I think you're attractive, but then I'm sure your wife thinks so as well. Look Steve, no harm done here, we can both walk away' I said. I was glad when I saw Allan. Steve stayed with us again through the second half of the auction but said very little. On leaving the auction room with Allan, Steve asked 'I'll see you next week then Russell?' 'Yeah see ya' was the only reply I could manage.

Allan was shocked when I told him, but not half as shocked as me. That night Steve phoned and asked if he could call around to my caravan so we could talk. I said 'no'. I felt it was better if we just met up at the auction if we ever had to meet up at all. The following week Steve and I went for our second wet lunch; it was just a repeat of the week before, only this time Steve said he was sure he was gay. I on the other hand didn't believe he was and I told him so. How could he say he was gay, he'd never in all his years ever thought about another man let alone kissed one. I agreed we could meet up on Wednesdays but as far as I was concerned we were just friends. The old dears back at the caravan loved it; of course I'd told them everything about Steve and to them it was the love story of the year.

Steve would call me every night asking if it was OK for him to call around to my caravan but I always said no. Then one night there was a knock at the caravan door. Opening it I was amazed to see Steve stood before me. 'Please let me come in' he said,'I cannot go on like this.' I was thinking that nothing had happened, but I didn't say that. If anything he was starting to scare me so why did I let him in?

Making his coffee I watched as he climbed on the bar stool that he had paid for, so he could sit next to me. 'I never thought I'd sit on this' he said, meaning the stool. I just smiled but was also thinking, that makes fucking two of us. He must have stayed for about two hours. I was trying to talk about anything but us. 'I'm tired now' I said. 'I've lots to do in the morning, I'm going to have to ask you to leave'. 'Oh yeah sure' he replied 'I'm sorry, I just wanted to come and see you, thanks for the coffee and thanks for seeing me tonight' I could feel the tension in the air as we both walked towards the caravan door. 'I don't want this' I was thinking, just then Steve took hold of me and kissed me, tenderly but quickly. I just stood there as he came closer for the second run. I could have stopped him but I didn't, this time it was full on and went on for what seemed like forever. 'I'll see you on Wednesday' he said, walking out of the van. When he'd left I told myself I shouldn't be having feelings for him, but I just couldn't help it, I was getting to like him. Getting into bed all I could think of was Steve. What was I doing?

The next day I told the old ladies hoping they could give me the advice I was looking for, but they didn't. They were loving it because nothing ever happened like this in their lives. The old dears were a rum lot and we all know what old women are like for gossiping; within the hour it was all over the caravan park that I was seeing a married man. Steve didn't leave it till Wednesday, and as I opened the caravan door a few nights later I must admit it was nice to see him standing there. It was a good job I'd cleaned up all the hair off the floor because this time as soon as he walked in he took hold of me and we ended up making out on the caravan floor. Considering he was a married man and he'd never had gay sex before, he was doing rather well. We went on like this for months. Allan had stopped taking me to the auction now that Steve was on the scene. My brother Tommy wasn't very impressed that I was seeing Steve and when he did meet up with him for all he was very polite to him he told me later that he didn't like him. I thought it was because of the fact that he was still married, but Tommy said he never liked him; 'Just something about him Russ', he would say. I of course thought that the sun shone out of Steve's arse; looking back it wasn't love but lust. I believe we've all got that one mixed up at some time or another.

Mr Jones didn't approve, but then he wouldn't would he? Most of the ladies were on my side and anyway it was about time I had a bit of fun. Wrong of me I know, but I didn't want him to talk about his family, maybe I thought ignoring them might make them go away; all I knew at this time in my life was that I'd found someone who wanted me for me, not because of what I'd got or what I could get, but for me and me only. Whatever anyone told me just didn't get through at all, I was in love and for once I felt I was being loved back and I liked it. Sod everyone else I thought. By now I was starting to see my own children often. I loved them coming over to the van but I knew they weren't too keen on the thought of their father living in a caravan, and I don't think they ever got their heads around it. I'd try to make it as fun as possible for them, but with no car we couldn't go very far; thank God for the beach and the local park, we always had a laugh there.

Tommy was still coming down every fortnight so we could do the car boots. By now Steve had started to pitch up right next to us, which was something Tommy wasn't too happy about. I on the other hand loved it, well I would wouldn't I, me being in love and all?

After the Sunday car boot Tommy went home as usual. I cannot remember how he'd done it, but Steve had managed to get away for the night, the whole night! He'd never stayed over before, and had always left before I'd woken. After a nice night in Steve and I went off to bed to do what gay men do best. The next morning I remember him waking me up saying 'I always have bacon and eggs for my breakfast' 'Oh do you now, well I'll go and make it for you' I replied.

Going into kitchen I thought Mmm I don't mind, I'll do it for him this once, but when Steve shouted 'two eggs mate' I didn't like that. Who the fuck did he think I was, his slave? Then there was the mate thing, nah you don't shag your mates I thought. I cracked open two eggs onto the plate, put a few rashers of bacon by the side of them then empted half a tin of beaked beans for good measure. Walking back into the bedroom Steve said 'that was quick' as he started to sit himself up getting ready for his breakfast in bed. 'I'm going for a shower now' I said as I passed Steve his food. 'What the fuck's this, it's not cooked? Steve shouted after me.

As I popped my head back around the bedroom door I said 'Oh sorry mate you asked for a full English breakfast in bed, you didn't think I was going to stand there and fucking cook it did you?' He just laughed, but I knew he was pissed off, as I got into the shower I thought that'll teach you mate!

It was a Sunday afternoon and the children had just been picked up by their mother. Everyone who knew me knew that when I had the girls over it was our time and no one ever called, it was nice to just have them to myself and that way they didn't see who was coming and going. To them I was just their dad, not a hairdresser, car booter or gay man, just Dad. Waving bye to them I could see Steve driving back into the park, but what was he doing here? He knew never to call when the girls were here. Pulling up in front of the caravan Steve jumped out of the car saying 'Quick, we have to leave'. 'What?' 'Look, just grab some things and get into the car, we have to leave and now, come on quick' he shouted. I didn't know what was going on, I didn't even have time to tell him off because he'd called around when he knew the children could have still been there. Locking the caravan door I shouted 'Oh shit, I've still got a quiche in the oven' 'Bring it with us' Steve shouted back. 'Now come on, let's get out of here'

Climbing into the car with my hot quiche wrapped up in a tea towel I had no idea what I was doing, or where I was going; all I knew was that for some reason we had to leave and now. 'I have a brother living in Torquay in Devon, we'll have to go there for now' Steve said. 'Torquay but why, what's gone on?' Steve went on to tell me that he'd told his wife that he was gay and that he wanted to come and live with me at the caravan. This wasn't something we had discussed and I wasn't very happy with him. What he didn't think about when he told his wife that he was gay and wished to live in a caravan with his new boyfriend was that his father-in-law was a sheep farmer; you know the type that carry shot guns. 'Oh that's just fucking great, so now I'm on the run from a mad ex-wife and a father-in-law who would shoot without question'. Driving out of the caravan park I could see some of the ladies looking out of their windows thinking what's going on now?

'Stop the car!' 'Russell we don't have time' 'Look, I've done nothing wrong here, I'm not running from anyone' Just then Steve screamed 'Oh shit, shit shit' The battered old van pulling up at the side of us must have been him. 'Fucking move, come on' I shouted.
It was a long way to Torquay but the journey seemed to go so quickly because of all the laughter on the way. All I remember saying was 'But I've got a quiche in the oven'. I had about forty pounds on me and Steve had about thirty and we had to at least get to his brothers on that. Oh well, I've never been to Torquay I thought, this should be fun. We pulled up to a motorway services, letting Steve sleep because of all his driving. This gave me time to think about what the hell was I doing? What had I got myself into this time? I couldn't believe I was on the run from a farmer with a fucking shot gun, and the best of it was, I'd never even met him. I knew my brother would go mad when I told him what was going on, and as predicted he did. On arriving in Torquay the first thing I did was call one of my ladies on the caravan park; I had to somehow try to explain what was going on.

I should have known she'd have thought it was great fun, and she couldn't stop laughing. She did at least agree to keep an eye on my caravan until I got back, but when that would be God only knew. By the time we arrived at Steve's brother's flat it was dark. Steve hadn't even told his brother he was coming, let alone bringing his gay boyfriend. To be fair his brother was really nice and quite understanding, considering what was going on. His girlfriend was a lot younger than him but she also seemed nice enough. We were just so hungry and tired by the time we got there, and with only one bedroom in their flat our first night on the run was spent on the lounge floor.

The next morning we all got up and went out for breakfast. As we ate Steve tried to explain to his brother more of how we had come to end up on his lounge floor. Again, Steve's brother was such a nice guy and said Steve and I could stay as long as we needed to. 'Well it looks like we'll be staying here for good now, there's no going back' Steve said to his brother. 'I'm not living here Steve, I've got a home and children in North Wales. I'm not moving here for anyone' I said. 'Well, we'll see about that in a few days, for now we'll have to stay here' Later Steve and me had a good walk around; the place seemed nice enough, but I was still shocked to think Steve wanted us to live there for good.

The journey had taken us eight hours so there was no way I could live that far away from the girls. 'We'll be OK' Steve said. 'For now we'll have to sleep on my brother's floor until something comes up' 'Oh, and when will that be' I replied 'Soon. Soon, you'll see'. That was the Monday and the first full day we were there.

That night as Steve slept I lay there on the floor thinking of all the things I had just given up and whether I really wanted to. The next morning I was up and out early. Walking past a nice salon in the town, just across the road from the sea front, I thought what a beautiful place it would be to work. So in I went. I was so lucky, as soon as I opened the salon door I got the biggest smile I'd seen in a long time. 'Hello' said the man who was standing behind the reception, 'Can I help you?' 'I hope so' I said returning a smile 'I need a job' 'Are you a hairdresser?' 'Yes, I am' and before he could ask me any more I'd poured out my whole life story to him. 'Well, I could do with a trim' he said walking over to the salon chair. 'Come on, give us a trim and tell me more, then we'll see what we can do for you' While cutting his hair the pair of us had such a laugh, it was worth cutting his hair just for that.

You'll Never Make a Hairdresser

'OK, even though I don't need another stylist I feel I'd be kicking myself if I let you walk out of here, and you'll only walk right in the next salon and they'll have you, then you'll become my competition'
'Competition is healthy' I joked. 'Yeah well not around here it's not, it's every man for himself, and you're now working here.' We just laughed. 'Listen, there is a flat above the salon if you want it, it's only small but it will do the two of you if you like it.' I couldn't believe how lucky I was, I'd only been out of the flat for an hour and I'd done a man's trim, got a full time job and now a flat. Steve was still asleep on the floor when I got back to the flat and he couldn't believe it when I told him what I had just got for us. Come to that neither could I. We moved into the flat above the hairdressing salon that very day and the following day I started work.

A week had passed and work was going well for me. That weekend I went out and bought us some things we needed for the flat. Steve seemed to be out a lot but said he couldn't find any work. The following Tuesday I'd got Steve an interview for a job in a casino. He got the job but he wasn't that happy about it as it meant him working nights. By the end of the second week I'd got both Steve and I good jobs, however as I was working in the day, Steve slept and as Steve was working at night I slept. I was missing my children a lot, as well as the old dears from the caravan site. In my heart I was knew the holiday in Torquay was coming to an end. I had ended up somewhere I hadn't planned and with someone I felt I didn't know. I couldn't say I was unhappy, because I was meeting new people through the hairdressing, but at night I was feeling very lonely.

I wrote to Mr Jones telling him where I was and how I'd ended up in Torquay. I also told him I wouldn't be going to see him any more. I felt I didn't need to; my appointments would be best used given to someone who he felt needed them. I thanked him for his help in the past and hoped we could stay in touch, but sadly we never spoke again. I was regularly calling the old dears at the caravan site and they were all missing me. However, the novelty of their friend running off with a married man soon passed as their hair started to grow, and before long they wanted me back home, with or with out Steve.

Steve was out at work one night or so I thought, when there was a loud banging at my door. It was Steve's brother who was screaming at the top of his voice 'I'm going to kill him, I can't believe what he's done' Following him into the lounge I didn't have a clue who or what he was on about. 'He's with her now, he's fucking with her now' he kept saying. 'Calm down, come on sit down, who's with her, who are you going to kill?' 'Steve' he shouted back at me. 'Steve's with my girlfriend' 'Yeah, he's been seeing her for the past week or so, he's never been to fucking work, he's been shagging her'

I didn't have time to think about me, all I thought about was this poor lad. I thought he was going to pass out as he was crying and screaming that much. 'He's with her now Russell, please believe me.' 'But he's in work' I said back. 'No he's not and never has been, he never even started his job' he said, still crying into his hands. Steve's brother also worked nights. That night while in work he began to feel unwell so went home. Getting home around ten his girlfriend wasn't there, so he called her on her mobile phone; no answer, so he took himself off to her mother's house. Her mother said 'She's not here but she was walking in town only half an hour ago, I saw her with your Steve. I did wave at them but they didn't see me. I was on the bus coming home from bingo'

I didn't know what to think. I didn't feel anything for me or Steve. At that moment the only person I was concerned about was Steve's brother. I called the casino and was told they'd never even heard of Steve. I had no choice but to go with Steve's brother when he said. 'I can't sit here waiting for them to come back, Russell, I'll have to go and find them' Getting out of the chair he asked 'Please, please come with me and help me find them.' Putting on my coat I realised I really didn't want to find them, if anything all I wanted to do was fill my car up with my new clothes and get back to Wales to my little caravan and my old dears; they won't believe this one, I thought.

By now it was really dark and there were groups of drunks staggering about the streets. I didn't like it, but Steve's brother was on a mission, he wouldn't stop looking; I believe we went up and down nearly every street that night looking for his girlfriend and Steve. 'Come on,' said Steve's brother, 'lets go down to the beach'.

It was already dark but walking along the beach was like walking blind folded, it was pitch black. The only lights we could see were in the far distance, and every now and then we'd hear the crashing of the waves. Then we heard laughter. We couldn't see anyone at this point but Steve's brother turned around to me and said 'it's her, that's her laugh, she must be over there some where', I still didn't feel anything for me or Steve, all I felt was sorrow for his poor brother. I really didn't want it to be her but sadly it was. As soon as they came into view Steve's brother went wild.

He grabbed Steve and they started fighting. The young girl just ran off screaming. I don't know why she was screaming as no one had said a word to her at that point. I fell to my knees on the sand, all I could see was Steve and his brother fighting, all I could hear was Steve blabbering like a big baby 'Please stop, please stop.'

I didn't want to watch or hear any more. I got up and started to walk home. For me that was the worst part of the night, not that I'd just found my so called boyfriend having sex on the beach with a young girl, but the thought that I had to walk home alone in the dark with all those drunks around. Walking home I thought, what am I doing here? Why did I ever come here? I had a life back in Wales; it wasn't much of a life but it was mine. I suppose that's what you get for running off with a married man and a half cooked quiche wrapped in a tea towel. By the time I got to my door I was finding the whole thing quite funny, but my heart went out to Steve's brother. The only thing he'd done wrong was to help out his brother and his gay boyfriend and that's what he got back in return.

Oh well, it was time to ring my brother; I knew it was late but as always he was the only one I could ever ring. Day or night Tommy was, and always is on duty for me, and for that I will always love him. Tommy went mad, but when he knew I was OK he said he'd drive down to Devon the next day to pick me and by things up. After a hot drink I climbed into bed. Steve was nowhere to be found and I didn't care what had happened to him or where he was.

I don't know how long I'd lain there for or even if I'd been asleep, all I knew was that I'd just jumped out of my skin because of a loud noise coming from the living room, which was right next to my bedroom. I heard the cupboard opening where the drinks were kept and knew that it was Steve. Mixed emotions came over me. On the one hand I was glad I wasn't being robbed, but on the other hand I could do with out Steve in my living room helping himself to drink. I just listened to what Steve was doing and decided just to lie still so he didn't know I was awake.

Not long after I closed my eyes quickly as the handle of the bedroom door started to turn. I listened as Steve made his way to his side of the bed, then lay there in shock as I could hear him taking off his clothes. Did he really think after what I'd seen and heard that night that I was just going to lie there and let him back into my bed? I don't think so; time to wake up.

I leant over towards the bedside lamp and turning it on said 'Steve, I don't think it's a good idea you getting in this bed tonight' Steve was standing there half naked, and by the look on his face I could tell he'd had one hell of a beating. 'Yeah I'm sorry, you're right, I'll go and sleep on the couch.' Picking up his pillow he asked 'Do you want to talk now or - ?' cutting him short I said 'You go and get some sleep we can talk in the morning' 'OK then Russ, good night' Steve said as he left the room. I didn't answer him, but one thing I did notice was that all my anger had turned to sorrow. I was now feeling sorry for him, but why?

I knew he'd done wrong and by doing what he'd done he was going to lose so much. If anything he had nothing left in his sorrowful life. For a start he'd lost his wife and children who I knew deep down he did love. His mother and father were surely going to take sides with his brother, and then there was his brother and not forgetting me, who up until that day thought was at the top of his chain; now I'd realised I was the last link at the very bottom, and at any minute I to was going to fall off. I'm sure to this day Steve just wanted to see what it was like to sleep with an other guy, but in doing so he believed he'd fallen in love. He should never have given me that bloody stool, I bet he's sorry now I thought. If he wasn't I certainly was for taking it.

I woke early. Looking at Steve sleeping on the couch I could see just how bad his face was; he'd taken a right beating, and for what? I didn't know what had happened with Steve's brother and his so-called girlfriend, but I'd decided I didn't care. In the time it took me to make myself a coffee my mind was made up, I was going home! I had to go and quickly, before I started to feel sorry for anybody else. To me, Steve had brought everything on himself; as for his brother, well it wasn't his fault his girlfriend was a slag and his older brother a twat. It was time I started getting my things ready to leave.

While Steve slept I began gathering my things together. I remembered my mother saying I would creep around the house like creeping Jesus when I was a kid, never making a sound (I wonder why). Well that morning she'd have been proud, I played the part off to a tee. Before Steve had woken up I had the whole fucking flat packed up and ready to go. I then went and sat on the outside step waiting for my brother. I knew it was going to take him hours to get here and I knew Steve would wake any minute. I wished I could have just gone there and then, because the waiting was making me feel sick.

I could soon hear movement coming from the living room and then the next thing he was stood right behind me. 'I see you've packed'. 'Yeah, I'm just waiting for our Tommy, he should be here any minute' I knew this was a lie but I wasn't going to tell him Tommy would be hours yet. 'Have I got time to have a quick shower?' 'Yes go ahead' I replied.

As soon as Steve had stepped foot into the shower I ran around the rest of that flat like a blue arsed fly getting what little stuff Steve had, and I quickly put them in bags by the front door ready for him to take with him.

After showering he placed a cup of coffee beside me on the step saying 'I won't be long getting ready and then I'll get out of your hair'. I didn't reply; I felt there was nothing more for me to say. The next time the door opened Steve said 'Well if you don't get out of my way I'll just have to stay here with you, is that what you want?' I got up and keeping my head down I moved to one side allowing Steve enough room to pass. 'Thought not' he said. By now he was stood on the top step right in front of me. For a minute I felt sick as I saw his hand move slowly up towards me and as it did it took the shape of a fist. Slowly rubbing his fist along the side of my face Steve said. 'I'm so sorry'.

I couldn't reply, I couldn't even speak. I watched him walking away with his few bags. It was a sad sight. By the time Tommy came it was getting late. Because he had driven for hours it was only fair to give him a bit of a break, so we went for something to eat and had a quick walk on the beach where I filled him in on what had been going on. 'I told you there was something about that guy, didn't I?' We did laugh; if only our Allyson could see us now or better still be with us now we thought, she'd have loved it.

After filling Tommy's car with the rest of my things it was time for us to make our way back to the caravan in Wales. I was so glad to get back home to my little caravan; I'd missed it so much and everyone associated with it. For the first few weeks I was madly busy catching up on all the hair appointments I'd missed; the old dears were lovely to me and whatever I did they were always there for me. But then they would be wouldn't they, having their hair done for just a few quid. I soon realised that I did miss one thing from Devon, and that was the salon I had worked in whilst there. I missed the other stylists, the younger clients, and most of all the money. It was soon time for me to see about getting another job nearer home, but I didn't know where. All that time I'd been away on my holiday in Torquay I hadn't touched any of the money I'd been saving for my car. I now knew I needed this car more then ever because without it I wasn't going to get the work I wanted; I just needed a little more money, then I could buy the car without getting into any debt.

One of my friends on the caravan site was working as a cleaner in a hotel in Llandudno. 'I can get you on with me if you like, the money's not great but it's better than nothing, that's if you want' By the following week I was working two hours a day, five mornings a week, all for thirty five pounds. I must have been mad. I would never get out of bed for that now, but back then I jumped at the chance. It was taking me an hour to walk there and an hour back, and by the time I'd done my cleaning job and got home, well let's say I was well and truly f***ed. But it was well worth it, within weeks I was well in with the owners of the hotel and instead of the cleaning I was doing their hair and getting paid for it. I'd then do their staff's hair and charge them too.

I'd been working in the hotel a while when I met a guy who had just been doing some work on a hairdressing salon in a town called

Prestatyn; he'd been putting some extra lighting in for the owners. He went on to say how nice the salon was and how he'd found the staff there so funny. 'I believe two gay guys own it' he said. Well that was enough for me. Nice salon, nice staff and two gay guys, what more could a woman ask for. Ha! Prestatyn here I come.

It must have been two or maybe three years later when I was walking out of Tesco's in Llandudno on a very hot day. Pushing my trolley back to the car I noticed a few workmen doing something to the ground not too far away from my car. As with most workmen their pants were half way down there arses. Walking towards them I caught sight of one of the guys bending down. I know that arse I thought, as I looked back to my surprise it was Steve! There he was, back in Llandudno working in a Tesco car park. I knew he was as shocked as me at what he saw, and who could blame him, I looked fab that day. We didn't speak, it didn't seem right him being with his work mates and all. I know he watched as I lowered the top on my new audi TT and drove off to Kylie singing 'I'm spinning around move out of my way, I know you feel me 'cos you like it like this, I'm breaking it down I'm not the same, I know you feeling me 'cos you like it like this!'
Thanks Kylie x.

Prestatyn

Prestatyn. Yes I'd heard of it, more than likely I'd been through it on my way to Rhyl as a child, when Sunny Vale caravan camp was the place to go. I believe a lot of families from Manchester and Liverpool went there with their children but Prestatyn, no I never remember stopping there. It wasn't hard to find, and once in the town centre I realised there were many hairdressing salons there but only one stood out. It was facing a big beautiful church right on the high street; this has to be the one, I thought. As I looked inside through the window I could see what looked like a young woman cutting a client's hair, but the more I looked the more I thought the young woman might just be a guy in a woman's dress; a very beautiful man I might add, but nevertheless it was a man. Dare I go in I thought? Oh what the hell, I've nothing to lose.

I told the young girl behind the reception desk that I was looking for a job and although they weren't advertising for a stylist I was just asking if there was any work going. As the young girl started to tell me there were no jobs available I could see the woman/man looking over and she/he just smiled. I asked if I could leave my telephone number and if there was any work coming up would she be kind enough to give me a ring. Taking my number she said she'd call if anything did come up. I'd only walked four or five shops down the high street when my phone started to ring. 'Hi it's Donna' said the girl 'I'm calling from the salon you just called into' 'Oh hi' I said 'that was quick' 'Seems there might be a job after all' she said 'Could you call back in the salon today?' 'I'll turn back now Donna and mine's a coffee with 2' I said laughing. Within minutes I was sitting back in reception with a coffee in hand off my new friend Donna.

'Hi I'm Dave but you can call me Danny, everyone else does' said the person in the dress who I now knew was definitely a guy. 'If you'd care to follow me upstairs I have a business partner that I'd like you to meet, his name's Matt.' As I followed Danny up the stairs, he explained that the salon was on two floors and the more I looked around the more I knew this was the right salon for me. I felt it was the nearest I was ever going to get to one that reminded me of anything like a Manchester salon.

Matt was a guy, but for all he dressed like a guy he acted and looked like a girl. They both interviewed me and apart from both acting and looking like women they interviewed very professionally. I did find it very odd to be interviewed by a guy in a frock, but what the hell, I got the job and that was all I'd come for, not to give out fashion tips to a transvestite. I went on to explain about my epilepsy and Matt said there wouldn't be a problem as his mother suffered from epilepsy, and as I'd be working with him upstairs he'd always be around (how lucky was I?) To start with they could only offer me part time work, but if we all got on and things picked up then a full time job might be offered. That was fine with me. It was agreed that I'd start the following Thursday. Only working part time in the salon meant I could still do the old dears from the caravan site because after all, if it hadn't been for them I would have gone under long ago.

Work in the salon was going well, the only thing I found difficult was getting there. If I got the train I was far too early and if I got the bus then I was too late. It was agreed that I could start work at ten and that way I could get the train to work. To be fair, the boys couldn't be any nicer to me and whatever I needed I got. This didn't go down too well with the other stylist, but as long as Matt and Danny were OK with it then I didn't give a shit what the others thought. Within a few months my column was full and once I got into work I stayed there for the day, unlike the other stylists who were in and out of there like yoyo's. Most of the stylists were self employed so if they didn't have anyone in they'd go home or nip out shopping. I always believe that if you're not there then you'll never build up a clientele. Every time a stylist said 'I'm just nipping out' I'd think yeah see ya, I'll have your clients, and take them I did. One by one each stylist lost their clients, and all because they wouldn't stay in the salon when it was quiet.

The two guys didn't know what was going on or who if anyone was going to turn up for work in any one day. Danny loved to paint, he was a shit colourist but give him a tin of paint and he was in his element. You'd go to work one day and the salon would be all pink, the next week it would be yellow and so on. Nothing surprised me while I was working there. I would have thought that Danny would have been more into flower arranging then D I Y, but no he loved his D I Y. I walked into work one day and Danny had laid a new wooden floor, the type that you clip together. Everyone complained, and some clients even said it was like trying to walk on a trampoline. It was making me feel I was sea sick, it was that uneven. It must have cost the salon a hell of a lot of money but that didn't stop them ripping it up the week after. It was a shame Danny had worked so hard, but it had to come up.

Matt and Danny had met at college and when they'd finished their hairdressing course they decide to open their own salon. They had been trading for five years when I got there and to me everything, apart from the painting, looked like it was working well, although I could see it was Matt doing all the hairdressing and as for Danny, well Danny was just happy being Danny and the clients loved it. They had both been living with their partners for some years and to me everything on the outside looked rosy. No one was more surprised than me when one evening Matt and his partner Terry knocked on the door of my caravan. After letting them in Matt said he had something that he wanted to ask me. Matt went on to explain that he and Danny were going their separate ways. He said that he'd told Danny the year before I came along and that they'd both agreed that Matt could leave as soon as someone good enough had come to take his place. 'Without you knowing it Russell' said Matt 'that someone is you'

'Danny and me couldn't believe it when you walked into the salon and asked for a job. Danny and I have agreed the date that I'll leave but none of the other staff know yet and Danny and I don't want them to know.' 'Then why are you telling me?' I asked 'Because' said Terry, standing up, 'Matt wants you to join him in the new salon as his right hand man so to speak. You can be employed, or if you wish you can go self employed and take 40% of your takings home.'

'But what about Danny?' I asked.' It's agreed between Danny and me that he will keep the salon, I don't want anything from him. All I want is the freedom to open my own salon. It's time I went on my own.'

I was shocked, but this was too much of a good offer for me to refuse and Terry and Matt both knew it. For me It was the next best thing to having my own salon again. Something that I never thought

I'd get back after my illness. It would mean going back to work full time, and for the first year Matt wanted to open his salon until ten at night. The only thing was I couldn't tell anyone, and the day Matt's salon opened, I would leave Danny's salon to start with Matt. I was told Danny wouldn't get any notice from me. I felt so sad for Danny, but I knew I couldn't say no. The wage I was being offered I knew I'd never get anywhere in North Wales, I'd be pushed to get that much if I moved back to Manchester.

I told Matt and Terry that I wouldn't say a word but that I needed time to think about it. Just then Terry burst out laughing, swinging his hands around as he looked at my caravan and said 'What's there to think about?, Do you really like living here?' Matt was quick to defend me and said ' How dare you say that Terry, yes he does like living here, believe me he doesn't need to.' 'Yeah right, I'll wait in the fucking car' said Terry as he walked out of the caravan. 'He doesn't mean anything by what he said' said Matt. 'Oh don't worry Matt, I'm sure lots of people think like Terry, people don't understand it when I say I like it here'. Walking Matt to the door I told him I would let him and Terry know what I was going to do in the next few days.

By the end of that week all I could think about was what Matt and Terry had said. 'Until someone good enough comes along, and that someone is you.' It made me realise that Matt saw me as his rival, and he knew if I was to stay with Danny his salon might not be as successful as he hoped it would be. I thought that if I let him wait for my decision he might just offer me that bit more, maybe 50%. Every time I saw Matt he kept asking me if I'd thought about it yet. 'Oh no Matt, not yet, but I'll let you know as soon as I have'. I was sure I'd get 50% or at least 45%.

I got a call at home from the salon, asking me to attend a meeting to be held on the following Monday. All staff were told to come along. On the way to the salon I was sure that Danny knew what Matt had offered me. When the staff were seated Danny and Matt walked into the room. Danny then started to tell everyone that he and Matt had decided to go their separate ways. Danny went on to say that everything would run as normal and that Russell would run the upstairs just as Matt had done. I sat there feeling so bad, and I didn't dare look at Matt. Matt's leaving date was set for four weeks on Saturday. Some staff cried, they didn't want Matt to leave, others thought it would be a good idea to have a leaving party. I sat there thinking 'I'm not fucking going'. The next time I worked Danny called me into his office and asked me how I felt about Matt leaving and how I'd feel about taking over some of Matt's clients?. He went on to say that it was the right time for me to go full time and that he would put my wage up for me. I said I was OK with taking on the new clients, but I also said I wouldn't be too quick to offer out full time jobs just yet, as I believed Matt's clients would more than likely follow him. 'I want you here full time Russell, there will be enough clients to go around, believe me'. Leaving his office, I told Danny I would have to let him know.

There was no one I could turn to for advice. I would normally call my brother, but he didn't know anything about hairdressing and neither did dad. The others in my family thought I was thick because I'd given up my sickness book to go and work part time, so asking any of them wouldn't have got me anywhere. This time it was up to me, and to be fair I didn't mind if Matt said no to every thing that I was going to ask for. I felt he wanted to close Danny's salon down and I knew he could, but if I was behind Danny he'd have a fight on his hands and he knew it.

That night I called Matt at his home and told him I wanted 50% before I'd leave Danny's salon. He just laughed and said 'there was no way'. ' That's OK' I said. 'I understand, but I wouldn't leave Danny's salon for anything less' 'That's fine, forget I ever asked you' said Matt as he put the phone down. I had nothing to lose by asking; if I stayed with Danny I was going to get a full time job and a bigger salary, if I went with Matt I'd take home 50% of what I was making, so either way I was set to gain.

The next few weeks were hard for everyone in the salon. I had started full time and was working really hard to try and hold on to the clients that Matt thought he would take with him. It was funny on occasions as I watched Matt almost run across the salon floor trying to get to a client before me. Danny was walking around like a lost soul, half the time he didn't know what day it was. The other staff were all walking around looking sad because they didn't want Matt to leave.

You'll Never Make a Hairdresser

At Matt's request we met up again one night. Both Terry and Matt agreed that I could have the 50% I'd asked for. I was told I'd also work up until Saturday night and then I'd start my new job on the Tuesday. I couldn't believe I'd got 50% off them when really I would have taken 45%. Now all I had to do was work for Danny until Saturday. Saturday night came and I felt really bad because everyone was saying their goodbyes to Matt and giving him cards. Matt didn't want me to tell Danny until Tuesday morning. 'You can call him from the new salon' he said. But as Danny gave Matt some flowers and a big card the words just slipped out of my mouth. 'I'm sorry Danny but Matt has asked me to join him in the new salon and I've agreed'.

You could have heard a pin drop as all the staff turned to look at me. Danny's face looked so sad as he walked over to me and held out his hand saying 'I wish you all the luck in the world in your new job Russell, I'm only sorry you didn't tell me earlier, now please get your things together and get out of my salon'. Turning to Matt, Danny said 'I think it best if you leave too'. That was one of the hardest things I'd ever done, but I felt It was better than just calling him on Tuesday to say I wouldn't be returning to work.

Within weeks the new salon was a huge success, and how could it not have been?. There were two of the best cutters in Prestatyn working there. Before long it was time for another stylist to join us. Allyson had been working for a salon nearby for the past fifteen years and Matt wanted her on board. Matt knew Allyson had a big clientele and he wanted them. Matt offered her the same deal as me and she came on board immediately. Allyson was a fantastic hairdresser, and I should say still is. Meeting her was one of the nicest things that had happened to me in a long time. I soon fell madly in love with her in a platonic way. We soon became very good friends and to this day if I ever need anyone she is the one I go running to. It's so nice to have a friend that I don't feel I have to ring every day just to let them know I'm still there for them. She knows I would do anything for her and I know she feels the same. I love her so much.

Allyson was such a good worker but it soon became clear that she couldn't stand Matt. For all he was a good hairdresser he was a terrible liar. I learnt to just ignore him and get on with my work, but

Allyson couldn't. Within four weeks Allyson was gone, and my love story had ended as soon as it had begun. I missed her so much. With Allyson gone it was back to just me and Matt running the salon on our own again. I'd just been given my driving licence back and I was so excited. For weeks I'd walked past the same garage with this little white rover metro sitting there. I'd pass it every day and each day I'd tell myself if that is still there when I get my licence then I'm having it. I'd been saving for what seemed like an eternity and today was the day I was going to go and get this little car which I felt had been sat there waiting for me. 'Would you like to test drive it?' asked the car dealer. 'No' I said 'When can I pick it up?' 'First thing in the morning, will that do you?' 'Oh that's fine, I'll be here' The next day I couldn't wait for that garage to open, and true to his word there was my little car ready and waiting for me.

I will always remember driving off. I was so happy, you'd have thought I was driving a Rolls Royce. I laughed to myself, because I'd been so eager to get my hands on that little car that I hadn't even wanted to test drive it, instead I just bought it and drove off! I was getting to a good speed when I noticed there was no fifth gear. It was too bloody late to go back, no wonder it had sat on the forecourt for so long. I didn't care really, I still loved that little car and to me it was a Rolls Royce, especially after not having a car for so long.

The long hours in work were beginning to get me down, and I couldn't wait for our first year to be up. I was still only having a Sunday off and every other Sunday I was having the children. There were times I felt so sorry for them because like all working parents, on your day off it's food shopping, washing and ironing. But the more I worked the better their stays became, a new T V and DVD helped a lot, as well as the car; all the things I would never have been able to afford if it hadn't been for my job. But the girls were always very good and very understanding. I knew when my hours were reduced that I'd be able to see more of them.

As we approached the second year in the salon it remained as busy as ever. I'd found us a cleaner to help out, but the hairdressers were not coming forward for the jobs we had advertised. I couldn't understand this; the salon looked fabulous, we looked professional, we had the right clients, so what was it? Why did nobody want to work in the salon?. Matt wasn't too bothered, he'd work day and night if he had to, but I wanted some time off and the only way I'd do that was if we got another stylist. I asked everywhere and everyone but still had no luck. Allyson had gone back to the salon that she had left to come to us and I knew she'd never come back. We plodded on in the hope that soon the right stylist would come along.

I was still in work one night when my mobile phone rang. It was Allyson.
'I'm the pub in town, I've found someone for you' 'Great, is he working now?' I asked. 'Oh he's not a hairdresser, he's gay, young, beautiful and loves older men.' I wasn't expecting any of this, but what the hell; we arranged to meet the next night. It turned out Simon was about fifteen years younger than me and as Allyson had said he went for older guys. I wasn't stupid, I knew it was only a bit of fun on both parts, but while it lasted the fun was good. Now I really wanted time off, so I cut my hours down to 6 O'clock on a Tuesday, Wednesday and Saturday. I knew it wouldn't be for long, but the nights with Simon were fun and until the fun stopped I was having those hours. This didn't go down well with Matt, but being self-employed there was nothing he could do.

I remember it all came to a head one night when Simon called into the salon. Matt was just leaving and as usual they didn't speak to each other. As soon as Simon and me heard the salon door shut we went into the stock room and did what gay men do best, when all of a sudden the staffroom door swung open. Not having time to do anything Simon and I stayed in our positions as Matt stood there shouting 'What the fuck's going on, this is not a knocking shop, stop what your doing and get the fuck out'
As Matt left the room Simon and I just started laughing. I know it wasn't the right thing to do, but it was funny.

The next day in work wasn't quite right, the atmosphere was very tense, but as always I just got on with my work. Simon was now spending more and more time with me, so I'd decided it was better to knock the late nights on the head and this also meant I could also have the girls over one night for tea. No matter how hard I worked Matt was never going to be happy, but I'd made my decision and was going to stick by it. As I thought, Matt went mad. 'We always said we'd stay open until ten at night and now your backing off.' I tried to explain that originally we both said we'd work until ten o'clock at night, but that was agreed for one year only, we were now into our second year. All week I tried to work as normally as possible but Matt was doing his best to make my life shit.

I'd agreed to stay later then planned one Friday night, to do one of my best clients. It was only a quick cut and blow and I knew I'd be finished and out by 8 o'clock .

With her hair done my client walked over to the reception desk whist I went to get her coat. While taking the bill, her bag that was resting on top of the reception desk suddenly exploded! I couldn't believe it. I immediately ran around the other side of the reception to see if my client was OK. Thankfully she wasn't hurt, just shocked like I was. The remains of her bag were now burning on the reception desk. I knocked it off onto the floor and started to stamp out the flames with my feet, when Matt came running over.

'Don't worry' I said, still stamping on the burning bag. 'My client's OK, her bag exploded for some reason'
I couldn't believe Matt's reply.

'I don't give a shit about you and your client, look at the state of my fucking reception desk, who's going to pay for that?'
My client and I just stood there in shock, when suddenly my client said 'I err I err, mmm' she couldn't get her words out because she was still in that much shock. Sitting her down I said I'd go and make her a coffee.
Matt followed me into the staff room ranting and raving about who was going to pay for the reception desk. I on the other hand wasn't thinking about the desk; all I was concerned about was my client, and as long as she was OK that was all that mattered.

Taking my clients coffee back I noticed there were two tea tree lights burning on the other side of the reception desk. As I looked on the floor there was a third which was bashed because of my stamping on the bag to which it had attached itself. As Matt came over I asked 'Who put the tea tree lights on the desk?' 'I did' he shouted back to me and my client. 'Well then, you're the one responsible for what just happened. If those lights hadn't been on the desk, the bag would never have exploded in the first place'

Matt went wild 'I want this, I want that'. I just let him rant on as I told my client she was OK to leave. I apologised about her bag and said I wouldn't charge her for the hair cut she'd just had done. I hoped that would be OK.'

Turning to Matt I said 'How the fuck could we charge her when it was you who had put the fucking lights there in the first place?' 'I want a new desk' he shouted as I walked away. 'Well you're not going to get one, get over it!' I replied. Then I heard those famous last words 'YOU'RE FIRED!'

I bust out laughing. 'What!'

'You heard me,' Matt said. 'You're fired. Now get your things and get out of my salon.'

Racing home I knew I'd have to call my clients that were in the very next day and as expected they were all OK with me. I arranged to do all my clients at their homes until I'd decided what to do next. I knew then it was time to open my own salon again.

With an empty shop found, I didn't have that much cash to go around, so it was all hands on deck. Friends, clients you name it, if they could do anything they did. I worked so hard in the six weeks before opening the salon. I still had to do my mobile hairdressing as this was the only way I could get any money to pay for the salon to be done. By the time the salon was ready to open there was no more money left; we didn't even have a float to top up the till. But as the doors opened the salon looked beautiful; the staff were all in uniform looking so smart, and more importantly the appointment book looked healthy.

Three weeks later I passed Matt on the high street. 'You have all your old biddies, and I'll have all the younger ones' he said laughing.

I didn't even answer him. I wasn't bothered who came into my salon as long as they had the money to pay. Within two years Matt's salon was closed.

What's that old saying 'What goes around comes around'?

Today we are still a happy, busy salon, and until I decide to stop, that's how it'll stay.

Johnny

I cannot remember the date but I know it was April 2003 when one of my clients Lisa walked into the salon to book a hair appointment. Standing next to Lisa was her friend Mr Jonathan White! After booking Lisa's appointment I remember Lisa introducing me to Jonathan. As I shook his hand I had no idea at that time he was gay. After a very brief chat Lisa and Jonathan left the salon and I went back to my work. The next day, and I can remember the exact time, it was four o'clock, one of my staff came up to me and said there was someone in the reception area. When I got to the reception there was Jonathan.

After a quick hello Jonathan said 'I can see you are busy, I'll call in again'. I remember walking away wondering what he wanted to chat about. The very next day, again at four o'clock, I was asked to go to the reception area. Again Jonathan was there. This time I sat in the reception with him for a few minutes chatting about work, the weather, silly things really, then it was time for me to go back to work.

As I was walking past Denise, the other stylist working with me that day, she said 'I think that guy likes you'.

'Who,' I asked 'Jonathan?'

'Yes' she said.

'No' I replied. 'There's no way that he's gay'.

'He must be' Denise said. 'He's not coming in here for a hair cut now is he?'

I couldn't wait for four o'clock to come the next day just to see if Jonathan would be back or not. Denise came up to me at four and said 'I can see that you're still busy with your client so I've asked Jonathan if he would like a coffee and he's in the staff room waiting to see you'.

I couldn't believe it, my whole body was going from hot to cold, my mind was spinning. Did he like me or had Denise got it all wrong? I was sure she had. When I got in the staff room there were so many people in there I just had time to say a few words to Jonathan before someone told me my next client was in and I had to leave Jonathan again go to do my client's hair. Believe it or not this went on like this for weeks, with me waiting for four o'clock to see if Jonathan would call back in just so we could have one or two quick words before I was taken off again.

I still wasn't sure if he was gay or not; all I knew at this time was that he was a nice guy and I was starting to look forward to four o'clock to see if he was going to call into the salon. Then on one of his daily visits Jonathan asked me if I would like to go out one night for a drink. The rest as they say, is history. Johnny and I moved in together in the following March. The time seems to have gone so fast as we both have very busy and demanding jobs with very long hours. We always look forward to our weekends and love going on our holidays together. We like to do something every six weeks, even if that means just spending the weekend in a hotel in Chester, Liverpool or Manchester.

People always say to me, I bet you and Johnny have a right blast when you go away, but the truth is we don't. We like to stay in nice hotels and go out for nice meals and as Johnny is up very early in the mornings we are usually up showered, fed and out walking by nine. After being out all day we're back in bed at ten. Walk and talk, that's all we do on our holidays, and of course we put all the world to rights. Ask anyone who knows us and they would tell you that we are so different from each other. However, I believe the longer we're together the more we are changing into each other.

I wouldn't have it any other way. Ha, just think by the time I'm sixty I may just have a brain as good as his. Narrrr, I don't think that will ever happen. Johnny is so intelligent, you name it, he has it. I'm very lucky I found him or should I say he found me.

Johnny is forever laughing at me (in a nice way I may add), he says I scare him with some of the things I come out with. 'Well I know what I am on about' I say. 'Yes, so do I. That's what scares me' he always replies.

I'm not to sure who asked whom but as soon as the law changed and same sex marriages were allowed to go ahead, we had the date booked. We had a wonderful wedding day and we were married in a castle in North Wales. Apart from the birth of my two daughters it was the happiest day of my life. We had planned it so well, just what we wanted. I did invite my family and to my surprise some of them came. It was so nice to see them again because it had been years since I had seen some of them and I was glad Johnny got to meet them as well. Everyone seemed to have a good time. It was so nice having my brother there as well as Bianca. Johnny's family loved it as did Johnny's mum and dad. The day couldn't have been any better.

Between us we try to do as much charity work as possible; From walking up Snowdonia to raising money for all kinds of different charities. I was so happy for Johnny when he was formally recognised for all the hard work that he does, and he was invited to attend a garden party at Buckingham Palace. We couldn't believe it; we stayed for three days in London, staying at the Hilton near to Notting Hill. We had always stayed in nice hotels before, but here was right where we wanted to be. We loved Notting Hill. We spent the days shopping, the evenings dining out, then back to the Hilton for drinks before bed. It was great!

We got a taxi to Buckingham Palace. We had been there before, but only as tourists. I had forgotten how many people gather outside the gates to the palace; whenever we have been there, there have always been hundreds. This day was like any other and the place was packed. When we got out of the taxi all suited and booted (I must say we looked fabulous) we had to make our way to the front of the crowds where the big gates were.

There to meet us were the Queen's guards. After checking our invitations they opened the main gates and asked us to walk along the red carpet that led us right into the palace where we were met by an other guard. We couldn't believe it, there we were walking thought the gates of Buckingham Palace onto a red carpet that would lead us right to the Queen. How mad was that? I'm sure the people outside must have thought that we were famous because as soon as the gates opened and we began to walk along that red carpet there were hundreds of flashing camera lights, all taking pictures of us. We just laughed. It was an amazing day.

I was so proud of Johnny and so glad I was there to share his day with him. As we were walking around the gardens we saw so many famous people, as well as members of the royal Family. It didn't seem real at all. Me, Russell Hughes from Wythenshawe stood in Buckingham Palace having tea with the Queen and with my gay husband chatting to all these famous people. What the hell was going on? I would have loved my sister Allyson to have seen this. She would have been so proud of me. Just as I was so proud of Johnny. This is just another experience I have Johnny to thank for, and there have been quite a few, but not all good I might add.

Being the boss!

I didn't enter hairdressing for the money (because in the beginning there was none) nor did I enter this profession because I felt it was all I could do with my life. I do feel I've been very lucky, sure it's me who has done all the hard work (I wish you could hear me scream the word hard) but I was very lucky In the sense that I had found out before I left school exactly what I wanted to do as a profession. Not that there was that much to choose from. I really don't know what I would have done if I hadn't found hairdressing.

A few years ago I employed a young girl as a trainee hairdresser. She was extremely talented. When her mother was told that she had been given a job in my salon she phoned me up and said 'Thank you so much for taking her on. She didn't do well at school and her father and me were so worried about what she was going to do. Then we both thought of hairdressing; we thought she'd fit in well with them lot'. Them Lot!

I tried to explain to her just how talented her daughter was but she wasn't having any of it. She was just so relieved that she had found someone to take her off her hands. I believe she thought she had dropped her off at the local mental home, the way she implied all hairdressers were thick. The girl lived in a council house with her mother who worked as a checkout lady and her father who was a bin man, and a very nice life they all had. After ending her training she stayed working for me for a few years before moving on to another salon.

Not too long ago I met up with this young lady who now runs her own salon and lives in a beautiful four bedroom house. Her mother and father still live in the same house and still work in their same jobs. Thick, I ask you?

I do sometimes wish I had stayed in school instead of taking off all the days that I did, but then I would never have found hairdressing. I must admit my job would have been made a lot easier had I stayed in school and at least passed some of my exams. I wish my reading and spelling were better. Some people find it very hard at school and sadly I was one of them. I did try, but no matter how hard I tried I just couldn't grasp it.

You'll Never Make a Hairdresser

Not too long ago I was cutting a doctor's hair when one of the staff came up to me and said.

'Sue's in for her colour. Can you tell me what to use on her please?'

'15 mils of 7.0 with 15mils of 7.3 with 30 mils of 6%' I replied.

When the stylist went away the doctor asked smiling.

'What the hell was that all about?'

'Oh I'm so sorry' I said thinking he was angry that she had interrupted us.

'No, no' he replied 'I found the whole thing fascinating; It was like another language. The young lady didn't even question you, she just went off to do what you said.'

He then asked if he could see the colour chart. I showed it him and tried to explain just the basic colours and what each one did. He said he had no idea hairdressing was so difficult. It made me realise what hairdressers take for granted and just how many skills we all have.

Whenever I employ someone who wishes to train as a hairdresser I'm usually able to tell you by the end of their first day if he or she will ever see their training through. A few years ago I started a young boy on a Saturday; he was fantastic in the way he looked, the way he spoke and the way he was with the clients. He was so good and everyone loved him. Tuesday nights were training nights, and even though he was only a Saturday boy he was invited to join in with all the other trainees. Out of them all he was by far the best, and at this time he was still only fifteen. He and I knew that hairdressing was definitely for him. Once he'd left school he asked if he could have a full time job to train as a hairdresser. I was delighted, and yes he was on board.

It was at this time I noticed he was very much like I was at his age. He had to be taken off the reception almost immediately. He might have been talented with his hands and worked well on the shop floor but sadly his academic ability let him down. In the appointment book Mrs Johnson was written in as lady, as was Mrs White and

Mrs Hughes. Mr Parry, Mr Thomson and Mr Smith were all written in as just gent.

This wasn't very good when the computer system asks you so many questions before it will allow you to book an appointment. I still wanted him on board and knew in time we could work on his spelling. After a short time the local college came in to sign him up so he could start work on his level one training. I believe when he saw the amount of written work he needed to complete just for the first part of his hairdressing course it put him right off.

I was not surprised when his mother called into the salon the next day to say that he had decided that hairdressing wasn't for him and she and his father wanted him to go back to college to try and get a better education.
'His father and me have always wanted him to be a doctor or a lawyer and never a hairdresser' she said.
The truth was she didn't even know her own son or his needs. I tried everything I could to get him back. Even the college were happy to help with his reading and writing, but sadly he never came back into the salon. I still see him from time to time when I go to the local market to buy my fruit and veg. I don't want to say what a waste because he is such a nice guy and maybe one day he'll decide to take up hairdressing again.

I have always had a good relationship with the trainees that I've employed. If they get past their trial period then they usually stay on for years. Sometimes relationships can be too close, which I'm told is my fault for allowing them to become friends. In my defence, it's hard working in such a close environment without all becoming good friends. But as I'm told time and time again you have no friends when you are in business, especially when they decide to move on.

I had a young girl working for me who was such a lovely girl. She came from a family who owned their own business in the Manchester area. I was asked by a member of her family if I would consider taking her on as a trainee hairdresser and I agreed. She turned out to be fantastic, managing the day to day running of the salon and as my right hand man so to speak, and although she got through her written work with ease, her practical work proved much more of a challenge.

I believe any other hairdresser would have finished her, but because of her organisational skills I decided to keep her on. We got there in the end and the day eventually came when she was awarded her qualification. Once the excitement was over I kindly pointed out that she had a lot more training to do and that the qualification she was given was for basic hairdressing only.

Thinking about it now I shouldn't have been surprised when she called into my office the following week to give in her notice. Her father wanted her to open her own salon and become a businesswoman like many of her own family. I tried to point out that only the previous Saturday she had been asking me to mix a colour for her and that today (Tuesday) she was telling me that she wished to open her own salon. I also pointed out that if I went away for a year I could walk back into my salon and it would have run as if I had still been there, simply because of her. But there would never have been a day in that year that she would have covered her own wage just by doing hairdressing.

'I am going to let you and your family use me, for one year. One because I like you and two because I know you are not ready to open your own salon'

'I can't, I open my new salon next week' she replied.

Her family had told her to leave as soon as she had given her notice which was 11 am.

'Will you stay until we finish tonight?' I asked, and she agreed.

At 6 O' clock I had flowers delivered for her and I gave her a colour chart that I had just bought for £390.00.I also told her she could keep all the holiday pay that I had already paid her. I did not want to ask her for it back; I was sure with opening a new business she and her family needed it more than me.

I wished her all the best and asked her to stay in touch. I was shocked that even though her family were in business they had told her not to give me any notice before leaving. All they had wanted was for Russell Paul hairdressing to train her. It didn't take long for her to get in touch. She would call me often and ask me how to mix a colour and, me being me, I would tell her. Everyone told me to stop telling her but I couldn't, after she was only a kid and had a lot to live up to.

Thousands must have been spent keeping her salon open. Money must have been coming from the other family businesses just so the family name could keep face; it certainly wasn't coming from customers because there weren't any. Sadly the salon closed. She did ask for her job back but because of her family I decided not to take her back. She began working for the family business in the office. I don't want to say I told you so, at least not to her, she was just a kid trying to follow her father's dream.

It's sad when good staff decide to leave, but then there is always another way of looking at it. As salon managers we must feel proud of the fact that once again we have trained someone to such a high standard that they have the confidence to open their own salon. Even if it is only over the road! I have always been told that competition is healthy. When some salons don't work out the stylist often wonders why. I've seen it so many times, there are some amazing hairdressers out there but not all of us make good salon managers.

I wasn't surprised when my eldest daughter told me she wanted to do hairdressing. I knew for a long time just how talented she was with her hands, and when I saw her drawings from school there was no doubt that she was very artistic. The only problem we had to overcome was that living with Johnny and I and working together as well might prove to be too much. Luckily though we got thought it. We would both agree it wasn't always easy but we tried to keep work and home as far apart from each other as possible. Of course this did not work out all the time, and poor Johnny would have to sit though his meal and all me and daughter would talk about was work.

I sometimes found it hard not to talk about work when I was at home with my daughter because although we worked in the same salon and most days in the same room I bet we only spoke once or twice a day for a very short time. If you think that every time we are with a client we are usually stood with the same client for an hour or more; if you have at least eight clients a day (and some days more than that) then in your eight hour day there wasn't much time for chatting. Although sometimes I felt I could scream at her for one thing or another, it is always nice to look across the room and see your own daughter working away and knowing that what she was working on always looked so good.

My daughter turned out to be a fantastic hairdresser (I know you're thinking I am bound to say that, but it is true). She would be the first to tell you if I thought she wasn't very good, daughter or not she would be out. Business is business, right!

Within no time my daughter had built up a good clientele and I have to say took many of my clients too. I didn't mind this as I knew she was good and they would be well looked after and it gave me more time in my own column which in turn gave me the opportunity to get new clients into the salon.

What usually happens when a new client calls up for an appointment is that the salon owner, if time permits, will put the client in his or her column first. After a while when the client has built up her confidence by regularly coming to the salon and meeting more of the staff, the salon owner will try and introduce the client to one of his other stylists, in turn freeing up his column again. The whole process then starts all over again. I have always felt that this is a good way to fill the salon up, and should one of the staff need to take a day off, then more often than not the stylists column can be split up between the remaining staff. The client would say if he or she would like to wait for her stylist to return to work, but usually someone in the salon would have at least done this client's hair before. That way both the client and the salon are happy.

Russell Paul Hairdressing was invited (in 2007) to go over to Spain and undertake some teaching for English kids who moved there and who were doing their hairdressing training. Bianca, Denise and myself were the three chosen to go on the visit which was to leave on the 5th October 2007.

The day before we left all the staff were working on the salon floor, when one of my clients came over to me and said.

'Doesn't your daughter look well, when's the baby due?'

I looked across the room to where my daughter was working and said

'Oh no she isn't having a baby, she's just put a bit of weight on'

After the client had gone I went into the staff room where my daughter was mixing up a colour.

'Guess what my lady said?' I said laughing.

'What?' she asked.

'She asked me when your baby was due' I replied, still laughing.

I should have known then by the look on her face.

'Dad' she said 'you know I love you, don't you?'

Shocked, I didn't want to respond at this time and I didn't want to say something that I would regret later, Instead I just said

'Don't worry about anything we will talk about it later, I have to go and do another cut.'

I was so shocked. My daughter having a baby; what the hell was going on?. As I was cutting my next client I kept looking over the room towards Bianca, and yes she did look pregnant. Why had I not seen it before?.

On a positive note Bianca was now living in her own house not too far away with her boyfriend. They both had good jobs, and even though I can say the timing may not have been right for all involved, at the end of the day it was very happy news. When I had finished with my client we both had a good chat, and as any father would I assured her that all would work out well. That night we had to get our things ready for the flight to Spain. The trip went really well and all the kids loved the new cuts that we did for them. They all agreed they felt much happier about the course that they were doing.

You'll Never Make a Hairdresser

I enjoyed the few days, and the opportunity I had to be alone with my daughter. Once we'd done the hairdressing part of it we had a good time. I don't think we had laughed as much together in years, so all in all it did us both good. Roll on the new baby!

There are many young people who struggle with lessons at school and who never find any practical skills to build on. Sadly they often get left behind and fall completely out of the system. I was lucky to have found a practical skill that would set me up for life. Looking back at my home life I realise that my own mother and father were not from an educational back ground.

If I was absent from school, sure they would shout at me but not because I was out walking the streets, but because the 'wag man', better known as the truancy officer, would be on their backs. If school hadn't been law we could have stayed at home helping them all day; they would have had us all off.

Mum was always bringing up young kids and dad was always at work or in his office (Pub), so in many ways I can't blame them for wanting us to go for the highest paid job even if it was in the local factory. For me to say I wanted to be a hairdresser was like saying I wanted to become a Hollywood film star. Where we lived people didn't do hairdressing, and I don't know of anyone becoming a Hollywood star either.

Luckily hairdressing has given me a very comfortable life style. No one has done it for me, and no one apart from me believed that I could achieve it. It hasn't and never will make me millions, but looking back from where I came from I can say I feel like a Hollywood star.

I did what I wanted to do and achieved more than I thought I would ever do. I have invited many of my own family over to Wales to come and stay with me and Johnny for the weekend, but sadly none of them apart from my brother and father have ever taken me up on the offer. I know Johnny is right when he says ask yourself why you are inviting them over and make sure you are doing it for the right reasons. I know he is right, but sometimes I just want to be a bit selfish and without actually saying it I want them to see there is no white uniform hanging up in my hallway. What I have I have worked for, and no matter what people say about you if you really want something that bad you can do anything.

You'll Never Make a Hairdresser

College

Love them or hate them we all need them if we intend to get on in life, or so I'm told. Personally I fall into the latter category, but that is just because of the experiences I had with colleges, or more to the point college tutors who were up there own arses and believed that hairdressing should still be taught as it was when Queen Victoria was on the throne. I believe that college is good for theory work, but all practical work should of be done in a real salon environment. If anything the tutors should question the salon owner about the reason why their junior is working in such a manner; yes Mr College, keep an eye on the junior to see how they are progressing, but I cannot understand how I and many other salon owners are expected to teach some aspects of hairdressing that we would never use ourselves to the young undertaking training.

All my hairdressing life I have had college tutors coming into my salons telling the juniors what to do and what not to do. I'd then pull the juniors aside to see what they were doing, only to be told that they were following instructions from the tutor. I felt the tutors were always ten steps behind the standards of hairdressing me and my team were working to. I remember a tutor leaving the salon one day in tears; I had a young junior that had only been with us for a day or two and had not been taught how to shampoo. She'd had a little go but never on a paying client. I was working away when I heard the tutor ask if she could watch the young girl do a shampoo on a client. My next client had been coming to me for years and I knew she wouldn't mind being the first real customer for the young girl.

I waited in the staff room while the client had her hair washed. All done, I walked over to her and noticed that the conditioner had not been rinsed out of her hair properly. I didn't mind and neither did my client as we both knew it was the girl's first time at shampooing, and with time she would get better. As my client went back to the backwash to get rinsed I headed back to the staff room.

Walking in I overheard the tutor say 'That was really good, I'll pass you off on your shampooing now, there you go you're ticked off.' The young girl asked 'Is that it, have I passed my shampooing, can I shampoo on the salon floor now?'

'Yes' the tutor replied, 'you've passed; you can now shampoo on the salon floor.' I had to stop this.

'Do you mind if I had a quick word with you?' I said, looking at the tutor. Just then one of the other juniors came into the staff room to tell me my client was ready.

'OK, I'll be out with her in two minutes,' I replied. 'Give her a coffee please'

Turning back to the tutor who was still sat down with the new junior I said 'I think that passing the kid on her first shampoo was a mistake, and I'd feel better if you took away the pass you've just given out until I felt she is ready to have it'

'I'm sorry' said the tutor smiling 'but I was more then happy with the girl's shampoo, so I feel it would be wrong of me to take way the pass away.'

I didn't have time to stand and talk all day with the tutor, my lady was waiting and I had to go, but I was dammed if the kid was going to be passed on that shampoo. It wasn't just about the shampoo. This tutor had been passing the juniors for years and I'd never been happy about it, I felt she was passing them on work they were clearly not ready to undertake, so much so that 'tick happy' was her name to all the stylists. Well today I'd had enough, tutor or not, that tick was coming off the girl's sheet.

'I take it you were a hairdresser before you went on to become a tutor?' I asked.

'Yes.'

'Well there was no way I could do a cut and blow on my client because of the amount of conditioner that was left in her hair, she had to be sent back to the wash basin to be rinsed again. I understand you have a job to do but I believe your main job should be working with the salon managers to find out at what stage each junior is at, and whether they should be ticked off yet. I'd like you to remove the tick from my junior and when I think she's is ready to have it she will.'

You'll Never Make a Hairdresser

I could tell from the look on her face that she wasn't happy with what I'd just said but I believed I was right; I knew I was right. Not only on this occasion, but for all the other times she'd passed my juniors on things that they couldn't do.

Still smiling the tutor said ' I do understand what you're trying to say Mr Paul, but the fact is I've already told the young girl that she has passed on her shampooing and I will not be taking that pass away.'

Turning to my junior I asked, 'Are you serious about hairdressing as a career?'

'Oh yes' the kid replied.

'Then can you tell me after working here for only a few days and after watching the rest of our team shampoo, do you feel that the shampoo you just did was good enough to have been passed?'

'No' the kid replied.

'There's your answer' I said to the tutor.

'But I never asked the question you did' said the tutor, still smiling at me. 'If I worked here I would have been happy with that shampoo.'

'Forgive me' I said quickly 'but that is why you'd never work here.'

'Oh, and why not?' the tutor asked.

'Because from what I can see you're a shit tutor and ten to a penny you'd be a shit hairdresser.'

Maybe I could of said it in a nicer way but the truth of it was she was shit at her job. I wasn't going to stand there and let her believe that she could ever work for me when I knew how shit she was.

As she jumped up her seat went flying back onto the floor.

'You can't speak to me like that; I'm here doing my job, how dare you talk to me in such a manner?'

'Well, maybe you're not doing a very good job.'

'I'm not having it, you will not speak to me like that again' she said, flicking her over-bleached hair back from her face.

'You're right love' I said passing her all of her books. 'I'm a very busy man, now take your crap and get the fuck out of my salon.'

Everyone went back to work, the kid ended up going to a new college and she became a really good stylist. Maybe I shouldn't have been so hard, but she'd had it coming for years. I believe the tutor moved to Australia with her husband, all I can say is god help them down under.

Years later I decided to go back to college and get my level 3 in hairdressing. One of the reasons for this was despite being a hairdresser for more than 25 years I'd never had anything on paper to say I Russell Paul was a hairdresser. When I started training you could go to college or do your training in a salon. I went for the five year in salon apprenticeship.
Also I wanted my daughter to do her level 3 because it would help her in the future if she ever wanted to go on to teach.

I have to admit I wasn't looking forward to attending my first day in college, but to my surprise I loved it, as did my daughter. Apart from enjoying the college we both had our best laughs ever from the situations we got ourselves into. I'll never forget the laughs we shared.

On a more serious note, there were things that I felt could be improved on in the course and like always I put my point across. To be fair the college did listen and I was still there to see some of the changes implemented.

The one thing that hadn't changed was the fear I felt as I walked into the classroom; it was like I'd just stepped back thirty years, only this time I was in a different location and with a different teacher. As the tutor passed out our books I began to feel sick, as she spoke I felt as if the room was tilting from side to side. I knew then there was no way I was going to get through this course. I didn't know if it was the classroom I was afraid of or the teacher. Put me in front of a mirror and I can do anything, sit me behind a desk and I feel sick.

I discussed this with my daughter but she was so keen about the course I felt I had to keep going, but all I wanted to do was hairdressing and not all the theory work that went with it; I wanted to hold a pair of scissors, not a bunch of multi coloured pens. My practical work was passed without any problems, but I was always being chased for my written work. Whenever I was given anything that looked like I had to read it or write on it, it went straight in the boot of my car, out of sight out of mind as they say.

The day the tests came was one of the biggest shocks of my life; for one I wasn't aware of the test. I'm sure I'd been told about it, but like most things that included reading and writing I wasn't interested.
Then there were the computers. I had no idea that all our tests were to be done on the computer, and this was my down fall. Although I was getting top marks in my practical work my computer tests were holding me back. The tutors noticed this, and although I could answer every question verbally I had trouble getting my answers over on the computer. It was then that I was asked to sit a test for dyslexia.

The day of the test I was full of hope. I was sure I didn't have dyslexia, how could I when I'd achieved so much in my life already? The results however proved I did have dyslexia, and by the end of the day it had answered so many of my own questions. Why couldn't I read and write like other people I know, why couldn't I hold the information that was given to me, why, why, why.

I was glad in some ways because I knew I couldn't have tried any harder when people said I was just thick, glad because I now knew the reason why I felt so sick every time I walked into a classroom or met a teacher. All those years before, when my old school teacher called me thick as shit, it was him after all that was thick for not noticing my dyslexia, and it was my school that had let me down.

Dyslexia doesn't stop you from having what you want out of life, it just means you have to work a little harder to get it. You'll find your own way around obstacles that are put in your way, but get around them you will. Whatever you do in your life you'll do well, or so I'm told. Remember there is never a right and wrong way of doing things, as long as the results are the same and you've done them the best way you know how.

Johnny's been good with me while I've been writing this book, although sometimes I believe I could have killed him. He's got more degrees and certificates than anyone I know, so as soon as I ask him how to spell something he'd say 'Let's break it down'. It's at this point I could kill, all I want is the spelling not a fucking English class!

Without the college I would never have got through my level 3 in hairdressing, and I'd never have known that I had dyslexia. For all of theses reasons I'm very grateful. But I still have to say, college tutors are good when it comes to paper work but as for hairdressing I'd send most of them back onto a working salon floor, and that doesn't not mean a college salon. Get them out into the real world of hairdressing.

Before I left the college I attended a hair up course; now to tell the truth hair up has never been my forte, but that doesn't mean I can't do it. After being given our clients to work on we were all asked to do a hair up style we felt we were good at. I decided to do a French roll. As I started to back comb my clients hair, one of the tutor's came up to me and said

'Russell I can tell you started you're hairdressing career in the 80's, we don't back comb anymore, take a soft brush and get rid of all that back combing please'

'But how am I -' before I could finish my sentence she said

'Just do it Russell.' Leaning over to my client she went on to say 'I'm so sorry, you sitting there with all your hair back combed to hell, he'll have it all out in no time'

With the back comb out, I started setting my trolley up with the hair pins, but I was thinking God knows how I'm going to get these to stay in. Just then another tutor came over.

You'll Never Make a Hairdresser

'Now Russ, what are you doing here?' he asked.

'I'm doing a French roll.'

'Carry on then' he said.

As I started to brush my clients hair over to one side, he said.
'I'm going to stop you there Russell. The first thing you should do before you put hair up in a roll is to back comb it, the more back combing the better'

As I looked at my client we both burst out laughing.
'What's so funny' the tutor asked.

Still laughing I called the other tutor over. With them both standing there I said

'I'm just nipping out for a coffee while you two decide to back comb or not to back comb.'

Walking out of the class room I could hear the whole salon laughing.

For those of you that want to know the answer it was to back comb. It just goes to show that not everything the college teaches you is right. Saying all that, I'm still glad I went; I met some wonderful people there, learnt lots of theory that I have to admit I didn't know or maybe through out the years had forgotten. I also found out I had dyslexia, which helped me to understand myself a lot more. As for the hairdressing side, I think they learnt more from me then I did from them.

I'd like to say a big thank you to three very nice people at the college I attended, you know who you are! Thank you so much. xxx

At the end of the day

While I have been writing this book It has brought back so many happy memories, but also a lot of sad ones that I thought I had long put behind me. When I think of the very first day I walked into Mr Quinn's salon and my first day at work; there have been so many lovely people that I've had the pleasure to have worked with. With these people I have shared many happy times and some sad ones too. You get very close to different people, whether they are staff or clients who have left, just moved away or have sadly died. I remember each and every one of them with very fond memories.

Johnny often laughs and tells me that I love funerals. This is not true, it's just that whenever a client dies I feel I have to pay my respects, and if that means going to their funerals with a bunch of flowers then so be it. Myself and Denise, one of the main stylists at my salon, often say we should look into opening a funeral directors next because of the amount of elderly clients we have between us, it would make sense to. Sometimes I have moaned about my job, or should I say the people that I've had to put up with, but I believe we all get fed up at some time or another. Looking back, I have loved the majority of my work. For all the shit that has happened to me in my life, if it hadn't been for hairdressing I really don't know what I would have done or how my life would have turned out. I dread to think.

I have also learnt so much from the people I have worked with and the clients I have worked on. I truly believe that without knowing it my clients have taught me so much and have led me in the right direction in my life. I want to thank them for that, as there was no one else to teach me the things I have learnt. I know it may seem mad, but they taught me things that they probably just took for granted themselves. One must work for what one wants out of life and not sit back and think that everything will just come to you. If at first you don't succeed get up and try again. Pay your bills; you don't have to live all your life in rented accommodation if you don't want to, buy a house and take ownership of your life.

I laugh now, but I remember being shocked that an M O T certificate for a car has to come from a garage and not the local pub, or your car tax comes from the post office and not from behind the

You'll Never Make a Hairdresser

local bar.

For all these things and so many more I want to thank my clients. The laughs I have had during the last twenty five years in hairdressing have been amazing. If only I could have bottled them up I'd have made a fortune. When I think that I have worked in places like Edinburgh, Manchester, Devon, North Wales, Spain and even Africa I believe I was right not to have gone for the safer jobs in our local factories, even though I would have had a job for life. Maybe if their hats had been a better colour, or Vivienne Westwood had designed them, then I might have just considered it.

Now because I have reached the end of my book I would like to say some very important thank you's. Although this may seem strange, I'd like to say a big thank you to Ozzy and Sharon Osborne because if I hadn't read Sharon's books I don't believe I would have ever sat down and taken the time to write a book of my own. Reading between the lines I could see what a wonderful couple they are, and more importantly what wonderful parents they make. I found Sharon's book so true to life; it was honest and above all I felt the love they have for each other and their family. I salute them both. x

Dear dad, so much to say but don't now how to say it. Let's forget the childhood for now; when I reached adulthood you treated me fairly and did things for me I never in a million years thought you would do. You respected me more when I was at my lowest and that proved to me that you truly were a good man. You have done things I shall never understand or forget, yet you have taught me things that I have used to enable me to get on in life. For most of those things I want to thank you.

Johnny, we have come so far in such a short time, the things we've done have been amazing. I never thought I'd find someone like you, and I bet you never thought you'd find someone like me (ha ha). When I first met you I was half way to where I wanted to be, but I still found each day a struggle. Thank you for carrying me the rest of the way; you made it so much easier for me. Thank you for believing in me when I was doubting myself; I'm so looking forward to the next forty years xx.

To my ex wife, thank you for giving me the greatest gift of all time.

My two girls, the days you entered my life were the happiest days I shall ever have; not for one second did I ever believe that I would have had two such beautiful daughters. You are two of the most understanding people I have ever met. Thank you for always being there, whether you wanted to or not, you never show it Xx. Bee, to say I was shocked when you told me you were having a baby would be an understatement, but if you were never to do anything with your life again you have made me the proudest father in all the world. You have a beautiful healthy son and as for you, you make a wonderful mother.

As you now know my sister Allyson died on the 9th of March 1997. I would like to thank God for allowing me to have been a part of her life and pray he is looking after her. Allyson, although you never gave birth to me, everyone knows that to me and Tommy you were our only mother. Without you Tommy and I would never have survived; I've heard people say 'I'd climb a mountain for him if I had to', but I will always remember the day you walked on broken glass for me, I shall never forget it, or you. I hope you got the job you were expecting. xx

Tommy, who is the other man in my life, I love you so much and could never thank you for what you have done for me. Without even knowing it you have saved me so many times. The inner love you have for others is amazing. So many people owe you so much, and I am just one of them. Thank you for being there for me and thank you for putting up with all my moaning xx.

Now this book is behind me I'm going to try and live my life the best way I know how. I'm going to carry on with my writing as I've got at least two more books that must be written. I'm going to continue doing what I love best; hairdressing, and I'm also going to put more time into the people who matter more to me; my family. I'm looking forward to enjoying the rest of my life with my husband, and then there are the grandchildren. I believe having grandchildren is better than having your own because we can always give them back; I'll let you know. Thank you all for taking the time to read this book, I guess considering my history, I'm doing rather well!

Now I would like to thank everyone from Mrs Johnson who spotted my first job, the staff I have working in my team now and every client I have ever worked on. I hope you have all liked your hair, and for those of you who didn't, always remember those famous last words; it'll always grow. X

I dedicate this book to my two daughters; remember anything you wish for can come true. XX

Lightning Source UK Ltd.
Milton Keynes UK
18 July 2010

157164UK00001B/17/P